# SPIRIT-FILLED
# *Preaching*
# IN THE 21ST CENTURY

# SPIRIT-FILLED *Preaching* IN THE 21ST CENTURY

EDITED BY
MARK L. WILLIAMS
LEE ROY MARTIN

Scripture quotations marked KJV are taken from the King James Version of the Bible.

Scripture quotations marked NASB are taken from the *New American Standard Bible®*. Copyright © The Lockman Foundation 1960, 1962, 1963, 1968, 1971, 1972, 1973, 1975, 1977, 1995. Used by permission.

Scripture quotations marked NIV are taken from the *Holy Bible, New International Version®*. NIV® Copyright © 1973, 1978, 1984 by International Bible Society. Used by permission of Zondervan Publishing House. All rights reserved.

Scripture quotations marked NKJV are taken from the *New King James Version.* Copyright © 1979, 1980, 1982, 1990, 1995, Thomas Nelson Inc., Publishers.

Scripture quotations marked RSV are taken from the *Revised Standard Version* of the Bible. Copyright © 1946, 1952, 1971 by the Division of Christian Education of the National Council of the Churches of Christ in the USA. Used by permission.

Managing Editor: Lance Colkmire
Editorial Assistant: Tammy Hatfield
Copy Editor: Esther Metaxas
Technical Design: Gale Ard
Cover Design: Michael McDonald

ISBN: 978-1-59684-778-1

Copyright © 2013 by Pathway Press
1080 Montgomery Avenue
Cleveland, Tennessee 37311

All rights reserved. No part of this publication may be reproduced or transmitted in any form or by any means, electronic or mechanical, including photocopying, recording, or otherwise, or by any information storage or retrieval system, without the permission in writing from the publisher. Please direct inquiries to Pathway Press, 1080 Montgomery Avenue, Cleveland, TN 37311.

Visit *www.pathwaypress.org* for more information.

Printed in the United States of America

# Contributing Authors

*Mark L. Williams* is general overseer of the Church of God.

*David M. Griffis* is first assistant general overseer of the Church of God.

*J. David Stephens* is second assistant general overseer of the Church of God.

*Wallace J. Sibley* is third assistant general overseer of the Church of God.

*M. Thomas Propes* is secretary-general of the Church of God.

*Timothy M. Hill* is general director of World Missions for the Church of God.

*Alton Garrison* is assistant general superintendent of the Assemblies of God.

*Hugh Bair* is senior pastor of Christian Life Church of God in Baltimore, Maryland.

*John A. Lombard Jr.* is pastor of the East Cleveland, Tennessee, Church of God and an adjunct professor at Lee University and the Pentecostal Theological Seminary.

*Marty L. Baker* is lead pastor of Stevens Creek Church of God in Augusta, Georgia.

*David E. Ramírez* is field director of the Church of God in Latin America.

*Oliver McMahan* is vice president of ministry formation and director of the Doctor of Ministry program at the Pentecostal Theological Seminary.

*Janice Claypoole* is pastor of the Ark of Mercy Church of God in Winchester, Kentucky.

*Thomas Lindberg* is senior pastor of the First Assembly of God in Memphis, Tennessee.

*Lee Roy Martin* is professor of Hebrew and Old Testament at the Pentecostal Theological Seminary in Cleveland, Tennessee.

# Table of Contents

## INTRODUCTION

Spirit-Filled Preaching Is Relevant for the Twenty-First Century
*Mark L. Williams* ............................................................. 9

## Part 1 — Principles of Spirit-Filled Preaching

1. Spirit-Filled Teaching Is Divinely Empowered
   *David M. Griffis* ........................................................ 23

2. Spirit-Filled Preaching Is Christ-Centered
   *J. David Stephens* ..................................................... 35

3. Spirit-Filled Preaching Is a Word From the Lord
   *Wallace J. Sibley* ...................................................... 47

4. Spirit-Filled Preaching Is Evangelistic
   *M. Thomas Propes* .................................................... 57

5. Spirit-Filled Preaching Will Have Signs Following
   *Timothy M. Hill* ........................................................ 69

6. Spirit-Filled Preaching Makes Disciples
   *Alton Garrison* ......................................................... 83

7. Spirit-Filled Preaching Flows Out of a Spirit-Filled Life
   *Hugh Bair* ................................................................. 97

## Part 2 — The Practice of Spirit-Filled Preaching

8. How to Prepare and Preach Expository Sermons
   *John A. Lombard Jr.* ................................................. 117

9. How to Plan a Sermon Series
   *Marty L. Baker* ......................................................... 131

10. How to Preach to Diverse Cultures
   *David E. Ramírez* .................................................. 145

11. How to Preach for Pastoral Care
   *Oliver McMahan* ................................................... 161

12. How to Give an Effective Altar Call
   *Janice Claypoole* .................................................. 181

13. How to Preach With Integrity
   *Thomas Lindberg* .................................................. 191

## CONCLUSION

The Uniqueness of Spirit-Filled Preaching
   *Lee Roy Martin* .................................................... 199

Endnotes ................................................................ 213

INTRODUCTION

# Spirit-Filled Preaching Is Relevant for the Twenty-First Century

### Mark L. Williams

I can forgive a man for a bad sermon, I can forgive the preacher almost anything if he gives me a sense of God, if he gives me something for my soul, if he gives me the sense that, though he is inadequate himself, he is handling something which is very great and very glorious, if he gives me some dim glimpse of the majesty and the glory of God, the love of Christ my Savior, and the magnificence of the gospel. If he does that I am his debtor, and I am profoundly grateful to him.—Martyn Lloyd-Jones

The heartfelt cry of the believer and the secular person alike in the twenty-first century is for a presentation of truth that will make a profound difference in life. In spiritual terms, that means a message from someone who knows what the Bible says and who shares it in the power of the Holy Spirit. The sharp rebuke of Jesus to the would-be preachers and teachers of His day was, "You are mistaken, not knowing the Scriptures nor the power of God" (Matt. 22:29). As in His times, the need of the hour is for preachers who know the Word and who deliver its eternal and unchanging truths under the anointing of the Holy Spirit.

That kind of preaching is relevant and life-changing in today's world.

*Scriptures are from the *New King James Version* unless otherwise indicated.

# The Calling

Jesus, who is the preacher's example, testified that He was called to preach:

> The Spirit of the Lord is upon Me, because He has anointed Me to preach the gospel to the poor; He has sent Me to heal the brokenhearted, to proclaim liberty to the captives and recovery of sight to the blind, to set at liberty those who are oppressed; to proclaim the acceptable year of the Lord (Luke 4:18-19).

Meaningful and life-touching preaching comes from the man or woman who has experienced a divine calling to be the messenger of God.

## The Call Assures Certainty

To effectively communicate the gospel of Jesus Christ, a person must have the assurance of a divine call. The call to preach is not occasioned by heredity, achieved by developing oratorical skills, nor conveyed by the hands of the presbytery. The call to preach is born in the heart of God and communicated by the agency of the Holy Spirit. The testimony of some is that the call even predates birth. The word of the Lord to Jeremiah explained that he had been sanctified and ordained to be a prophet from his mother's womb (Jer. 1:5). Isaiah, too, wrote, "The Lord has called Me from the womb" (Isa. 49:1). Paul the apostle said, "It pleased God, who separated me from my mother's womb and called me through His grace, to reveal His Son in me, that I might preach Him among the Gentiles" (Gal. 1:15-16).

Scripture is replete with biographical data of preachers and prophets and how they came to discover God's sovereign call. Samuel awakened to his call when he learned to distinguish between the voice of God and that of Eli. Moses heard his call during a crisis encounter with God late in life while standing barefoot before a burning bush. To Isaiah, the call came through a divine revelation of the Lord in the Temple in the year that King Uzziah died. Paul had an encounter with the resurrected Christ while journeying on a road to Damascus. Each calling was unique, but all were divine and directional.

It is the same today. God still calls men and women to the sacred service of delivering His Word. It comes in various forms and under differing circumstances; nevertheless, His call is certain and specific. Often the sense of calling is overwhelming, accompanied by a burden and evidenced by fruit.

### The Call Is Personal

How do you know if you are called to preach? For me, the call of God can best be described as an unmistakable, inescapable, irresistible, inner compulsion and constraint; a sense of absolute urgency and necessity to preach the gospel of Jesus Christ. Scripturally, it is probably best expressed by Paul: "For if I preach the gospel, I have nothing to boast of, for necessity is laid upon me; yes, woe is me if I do not preach the gospel!" (1 Cor. 9:16).

The call of God came to me on Sunday night, November 23, 1983, at the Conn Center on the Lee University campus. I had transferred to Lee from the University of Denver as a premed major on an academic scholarship, hoping to complete my studies, continue to medical school, and become a cardiovascular surgeon. But God had other plans for me.

On the surface, things were going great for me, but inwardly I was miserable and dying. That Sunday night in chapel, Lee president Dr. Ray H. Hughes preached a sermon on Calvary, "What Does the Cross Mean to You?" As the Holy Spirit brought me face-to-face with the Cross, I saw Jesus in all the glory of His passion. I saw myself and all my pitiful attempts to direct my own life. But I also saw a world that was lost and hopelessly dying. In broken repentance I cried out, "God, why do You need me? You have Ray Hughes, T. L. Lowery, Billy Graham, Steve Brock, and all those other preachers. I have no talent, nothing to offer You. But if You will help me to hide Your Word in my heart, I will go where You want me to go, I will be what You want me to be, I will say what You want me to say."

With simplicity and sincerity, I accepted God's call, and that vivid experience—as real to me as my conversion—has served as a point of reassurance through years of ministry.

In my understanding, the call to preach follows a Trinitarian formula: The authority to preach comes from God the Father ("As the Father has sent Me, I also send you" [John 20:21]); the message preached is Jesus Christ as Savior and Lord; and the power for preaching is the anointing of the Holy Spirit. This frames a theology of preaching that encompasses the God who speaks, the Son who saves, and the Spirit who empowers.

**The Call Requires Obedience**

For me, the apostle Paul is "Exhibit A" for what the preacher ought to be and do. Both in his own ministry and in his instructions to the young preachers who learned from him, he kept preaching central. He realized clearly that his principal task as a messenger of Christ was to present the gospel with the purpose of winning followers of Christ.

Listen to his heart as he says in Romans 9:2-3: "I have great sorrow and continual grief in my heart. For I could wish that I myself were accursed from Christ for my brethren, my countrymen according to the flesh." Feel his burden in 10:1: "Brethren, my heart's desire and prayer to God for Israel is that they may be saved." Take note of his approach in 1 Corinthians 9:22: "To the weak I became as weak, that I might win the weak. I have become all things to all men, that I might by all means save some." Hear his intent as he writes to the wealthy Christian who had a church in his house: "I appeal to you for my son Onesimus, whom I have begotten while in my chains, who once was unprofitable to you, but now is profitable to you and to me. I am sending him back. You therefore receive him, that is, my own heart"

(Philem. 1:10-12). This is the heartbeat of a God-called preacher who understands the evangelistic dimensions of his assignment.

He commended preaching to those with whom he ministered. To Titus he emphasized the necessity of "holding fast the faithful word" (Titus 1:9 NASB). His counsel to this young preacher he had left in charge of the churches in Crete was, "Exhort in sound doctrine and . . . refute those who contradict" (v. 9 NASB). To Timothy in Ephesus he wrote: "In the face of devilish doctrines, don't compromise the message. Don't bend. Don't bow. Don't back up. Don't be intimidated. Don't hesitate to declare the whole counsel of God. Keep preaching the Word. Be faithful to the message to which you have been called. Refuse to tickle itching ears. Reprove, rebuke, exhort with all longsuffering and doctrine" (2 Tim. 4:2-5, paraphrased).

The idea behind "itching ears" (v. 3) is that of entertainment. Some people want their ears tickled with sensational, stimulating oratory—messages that tell them what they want to hear rather than what God wants them to hear.

It is for such a time as this, and to a world such as this, that you and I have been called to stand and announce, "The Spirit of the Lord is upon me, because He has anointed me to preach the gospel" (see Luke 4:18).

## The Challenge

The mission of the Church of God is to proclaim the full gospel of Jesus Christ in the Spirit and power of Pentecost. The question is, how can we faithfully and effectively communicate a first-century message to a twenty-first-century world?

The preaching of the Cross is foolishness to those who are perishing. Yet God has chosen the foolish things of the world to confound the wise. The fulfillment of the Great Commission depends on giving faithful witness to God's saving work through

Jesus Christ. "Whoever calls on the name of the Lord shall be saved," but how shall they hear and believe without a preacher (see Rom. 10:13-14)? Never has there been a greater need for a preacher and the preached Word of God by the power of the Spirit than today.

Voices arise from time to time suggesting there ought to be a better way to communicate the gospel than preaching. Surely with all the new technology that exists, they say, someone should come up with a new way for the church to maintain itself and proclaim its message. But, according to Scripture, "It pleased God by the foolishness of preaching to save them that believe" (1 Cor. 1:21 KJV). Preaching is God's plan. Those who look for an alternative are usually young believers who do not know better, or old believers with poor memories.

**The Context of the Preacher's Ministry**

The world's complexity is increasing at exponential speed. Political alliances are in a constant state of flux. Threats of nuclear and biological terrorism have become frequent occurrences. A downturn in the global economy monetarily devastates nations overnight. The twenty-first century has brought a morally bankrupt climate into an era marked by paradigm shifts, geopolitical changes, and environmental concerns.

The speed of change has accelerated dramatically, especially in the world of technology. A billion web pages are available online, 65,000 apps may be downloaded to iPhones, 10,500 radio stations broadcast daily, and more than 200 cable networks are accessible. In the United States, 240 million television sets may be viewed by people, including 2 million mounted in bathrooms! The average teen receives 2,272 telephone text messages each month. What is worse, these statistics are already two years old at the time of this book's publication! The computer in today's typical cell phone is a million times cheaper, a thousand times more powerful, and a hundred thousand times smaller than the one computer that existed at Massachusetts Institute of

Technology in 1965. Knowledge is advancing so rapidly that it is difficult to know how quickly it doubles; some say it doubles every two years. At some future date, if Jesus does not return to earth soon, someone will pick up this book and smile at how outdated these statements will seem.

The people who listen to today's preachers have largely embraced secular humanism and moral relativism, and they hear there is no such thing as unchanging truth. The powerful people today are those who control information, and this raises concerns among thinking people. They recognize the rising debt and fragile economy—and they worry. They see the rising crime rate and rampant lawlessness—and they worry. They acknowledge the drug crisis, the AIDS epidemic, and the threat of pandemics—and they worry. They realize that society is increasingly secular, racial division is widespread, physical and sexual violence is unbridled—and they worry.

Since Adam's fall, this has been a world in rebellion against God. The insurrection has not caught God by surprise, however, and He has never written off the possibility of man's return to Him. Through the eons, He has sent His spokesmen to declare His Word.

Into such a complex, complicated, and confused setting today, God still commissions His messengers.

## The Source of the Preacher's Message

The preacher's text is the Book. Preaching comes alive when the preacher has so immersed himself in the atmosphere of the Bible until that world where God is alive and active becomes his world. It will offer him no end of sermon texts and stories and illustrations and real-life lessons. It is an unseen spring at the bottom of the well that never runs dry and keeps the well full no matter how much water is taken out.

Pointing back to the Bible creates a dilemma for today's pulpit. The people who show up at church and sit in the pews on Sunday morning are a different crowd than those who attended church in previous years. With the exception of those relatively few who have been brought up in church, the typical worshipers or church visitors are likely to be biblically illiterate. Many have never heard of baby Moses in the bulrushes. They have never read of fearless David and his sling. They don't know about dreaming Joseph. And if they have heard about Jonah and the whale, it is considered by them to be the biggest fish tale ever told. Unconverted men and women have been schooled by the liberal educational environment in which they were shaped to believe truth is relative, not absolute; ethics is situational, not fixed; and morality is as changeable as the clothes they wear. Their philosophy is existential: they live for the here and now, just for a short time, on a planet that they believe appeared after a "big bang," aimless and purposeless, without meaning. The concept of sin is likely to be foreign to them.

The preacher's task is daunting.

# The Delivery

A striking statement from Martin Luther accentuates the importance of the preached Word:

> If a hundred thousand Christs had been crucified and no one said anything about it, what use would that have been? Just betrayal to the cross. . . . We must draw this deed into history and divulge it to the whole world . . . to the deed must be added the use made of the deed, that it may be proclaimed by the word, held by faith, and that he who believes may be saved.

The "good news" is not good news unless people hear it. The charge God gives to His servants is "Preach the Word." What goes into the fulfillment of this marvelous commission?

## Start With Relationships

Second only to the consciousness of a divine call is the need for intimacy with Jesus. It is the overflow of the heart that gives the lips full speech. Communion with God in prayer and consistent Bible study is not only elemental for effective preaching, but absolutely essential for a productive life. Jesus' call to His disciples was "that they might be with Him and that He might send them out to preach" (Mark 3:14). The implication? "Being with Him" was a prerequisite for preaching "for Him." Ministry originates and flows out of fellowship with Him.

Deepen your divine relationship by devotion. The richer a preacher's devotion, the richer the sermons. A caveat must be sounded at this point: Do not use prayer and Bible study as a means to an end. Too many ministers have succumbed to the trap of using devotional time as an occasion to search out sermon ideas and texts. Spending precious time with the Lord is not a means to an end, unless He is considered the end. However, as you spend time in His presence, the Holy Spirit will illumine and apply the Word of God to your life. He will give you insight into the truths of Scripture or will bring to your mind a particular need in your own life or in the congregation to which you preach. Without conscious intention, messages will spring to your thoughts.

The preacher's relationship is not only with God, but also with the people to whom the sermon is addressed. The venerable James Stewart, a Scot, was fond of saying, "Every message must begin in Jerusalem and end in Aberdeen, or else begin in Aberdeen and end in Jerusalem." What he was saying, of course, was that the sermon must begin or end in the Bible and must have relevance to the town, the people who are listening. When the preacher is a pastor, as most are, his or her sermons ought to be addressed to the needs of the congregation, needs that will be recognized only if there is a meaningful relationship between the pastor and the congregants.

While there are universal needs to which messages must be addressed, it is also true that specific situations warrant attention from the pulpit. Has the community suffered a recent tragedy? Is the congregation sufficiently involved in the world mission of the church? Have world or local situations caused a spirit of fear to settle over the people? Does a moral issue in the news need a biblical perspective? Is there a need for healing . . . for correction . . . for baptism in the Spirit? A pastor who cares and interacts and nurtures a relationship with the people of the church will pick up on themes that require attention. Praying, fasting, and simply living among the people will bring revelation.

### Anointing Makes the Difference

One of my preaching mentors, Ray H. Hughes, repeated a sermon that ministered powerfully to his hearers, titled "The Anointing Makes the Difference," and he demonstrated it in his own pulpit ministry. His declaration about the need of the unction of the Holy Spirit reflects the insight of the nineteenth-century "Prince of Preachers," Charles H. Spurgeon, who wrote:

> The gospel is preached in the ears of all men; it only comes with power to some. The power that is in the gospel does not lie in the eloquence of the preacher; otherwise, men would be converters of souls. Nor does it lie in the preacher's learning; otherwise, it could consist of the wisdom of men. We might preach till our tongues rotted, till we should exhaust our lungs and die, but never a soul would be converted unless there were [a] mysterious power going with it—the Holy Ghost changing the will of man. O sirs! We might as well preach to stone walls as preach to humanity unless the Holy Ghost be with the word, to give it power to convert the soul.

A preacher can have excellent form and content, but if the message preached is not delivered effectively, it can fall on deaf and unresponsive ears. For this reason, special care must be given to delivery technicalities so the earthen vessel will not taint or distract from the treasure of the gospel within.

No discussion of preaching is complete without attention given to the length of the sermon. Let me go on record as saying that the length of the sermon is not as important as some people think. I've sat through sermons that lasted more than an hour, and when the preacher was finished, I still wanted more. That does not suggest, however, that a preacher ought to engage in ministerial filibusters. I like the counsel given to preachers in general: "If you haven't struck oil after a while, quit boring!"

Preachers need to be aware that by the time today's generation reaches adulthood, the typical individual has watched more than twenty-four thousand hours of television. The great majority of the programs last thirty minutes, during which a situation is presented, dealt with, and solved. The thirty minutes are broken up into five-to-seven minute segments, interrupted by commercials, during which the attention is disrupted. Today's adults, especially young adults, have been conditioned in this manner to have short attention spans. The wise preacher, recognizing this reality, will change the pace of the sermon at intervals, "interrupting" himself to insert an illustration, possibly a humorous statement, or at least an alteration of voice, lowering or raising volume or tempo.

In a "Twitter" world, where the text transmission allows only 140 typed characters, it is a brave preacher who attempts extended sermons.

## Fighting Bees

Abraham Lincoln observed, "When I hear a man preach, I like to see him act as if he were fighting bees." While I'm not too fond of the metaphor, I know what Lincoln meant. Nothing can throw water on a sermon more than a listless, stodgy, dry delivery. I've heard T. L. Lowery quote Vance Havner's assertion, "Some preachers ought to put more fire into their sermons, or more of their sermons into the fire." The difference between traditional historic Protestant preaching and Pentecostal preaching, someone has observed, is that "they have the truth on ice and Pentecostals have it on fire."

Preaching that is not exciting—and, please understand, I'm not advocating some kind of rote platform gymnastics—will not attract and keep a congregation. We call what we deliver *the gospel*, which means "good news." Delivering good news does not call for objectively stating a proposition; on the contrary, it ought to seem more like shouting a headline.

More and more, it seems to me that what is required in a preacher is a sense of drama. When the man behind the pulpit possesses this almost indefinable quality, he is able to help his hearers grasp the movement, the excitement of the message. A speaker who does not have it might as well be reciting pages of a dead, dusty, dry philosophy. The teaching and preaching of Jesus was not about ideas as ends in themselves as much as it was about attitudes that are rooted in experience. The New Testament message was all about movement, action. Paul, whom we think of as a learned academic, is revealed not so much a man of the study as a man of the road.

I think of the preacher's task as being similar to that of a museum guide. Recently, I was walking through a museum with nothing but the small signs in front of each display to inform me about the exhibits. Up ahead, a guide was walking with a small group, explaining the significance of what they were seeing. He permitted my family and me to join. He was showing each treasure, describing its origin, telling about its background, elucidating the richness of its meaning. The guide opened up a whole new world in the museum for me! I was now grasping a new dimension about what I was seeing that I could never have realized on my own. An effective preacher will do that for his or her listeners.

The preacher must perform ministry with some level of excitement. Gerald Kennedy, a popular Methodist leader of the last generation, wrote about a bishop who visited the church of one of his young pastors and heard him speak. Afterward, they sat together in the pastor's study. "I'll let you rest," said the bishop. "You must be tired after preaching."

"No," responded the pastor, "I never get tired when I preach."

The bishop answered, "Son, when a man preaches, somebody gets tired."

Weariness after a message gives no assurance that the preaching has been effective, but if the preacher engages emotional strength in the delivery, he will likely feel emotionally wrung out when he has finished.

## The End of the Matter

There is so much more that needs to be said about relevant preaching beyond this cursory introduction, and I am grateful that many have taken in hand to expound on the subject at great length. I have benefited from many books on preaching, and I hope my writing reflects the good I have taken from them. The book you hold in your hand is designed to help us take next steps and keep improving on the craft to which God has called us. The following chapters will share issues about the principles and practices of preaching. I commend these pages to your learning and application.

My personal counsel comes to you in the words of the seventeenth-century French churchman Francois Fénelon: "I would have every minister of the gospel address his audience with the zeal of a friend, with the generous energy of a father, and with the exuberant affection of a mother."

Nothing honors God more than the faithful declaration of His truth. May He bless you richly as you practice this prime means of grace.

# 1

# Spirit-Filled Teaching Is Divinely Empowered

### David M. Griffis

*For after that in the wisdom of God the world by wisdom knew not God, it pleased God by the foolishness of preaching to save them that believe. For the Jews require a sign, and the Greeks seek after wisdom; but we preach Christ crucified, unto the Jews a stumbling block, and unto the Greeks foolishness; but unto them which are called, both Jews and Greeks, Christ the power of God, and the wisdom of God* (1 Cor. 1:21-24).

God has proven Himself to be a decisive and sovereign God. He has established rules, laws, and principles that both guide and guard the events of the universe. He has declared Himself to be unchangeable: "For I am the Lord, I change not" (Mal. 3:6). The psalmist declared, "Our God is in the heavens: he hath done whatsoever he hath pleased" (115:3).

In His divine wisdom, God decided He would use the "foolishness of preaching" to save the world. The apostle Paul explained why God chose this method—God wanted to use simple or base things to "confound the wise" (1 Cor. 1:27), for even the "foolishness of God" is wiser than human wisdom of men (v. 25). Paul reminded the Corinthians, some of whom evidently were called into the ministry, that God did not necessarily call the wise or the mighty or the noble to preach the gospel, but rather He called simple vessels. Then when these vessels were

*Scriptures are from the King James Version.

anointed and used mightily to proclaim the powerful and productive gospel, no flesh would glory (vv. 26-29). Any wisdom, righteousness, sanctification (holiness), or redemption that we have as vessels comes from the Lord, and only in Him should we glory (vv. 30-31).

For centuries, the church of the Lord Jesus Christ experienced the gleaning of the harvest and the molding of the body of Christ through the preaching of the Word. History is filled with examples of men and women who allowed themselves to be instruments called *preachers*. No one questioned the method. God had stated plainly that preaching was His chosen method. Certainly other talents and gifts operated in the church, and God used a host of multitalented and gifted people; but for centuries it was understood that God's chief method to convict men and women of sin and to spread the truth of Jesus Christ was preaching.

God has placed many gifts in the church as He willed (1 Cor. 12:11). Certainly, diversity beautifies the body of Christ. It never ceases to amaze me how God distributes the workload of the church among diverse types of people.

And let me say emphatically, God can use a multiplicity of programs, a menagerie of electronic and computerized equipment, creative study groups of every nature, and masterfully written plays and songs of all sorts. After all, if God used a storm, a whale, a gourd vine, and a worm to teach the prophet Jonah object lessons about mercy, forgiveness, and the importance of lost souls, He can use twenty-first-century gadgetry for His purposes. He who made the sun to stand still in Joshua's day to defeat the Amorites can use a DVD player to help a group of four-year-olds sit still long enough to learn about God's love.

**Dangerous Cynicism**

The danger is not in programs or methods to train and equip the church. The danger lies in a cynicism that is developing toward preachers and the preaching of the gospel. What has brought this on? I believe this attitude is a wound that has been received in last-day spiritual warfare. What caused this grievous wound?

*First, we have witnessed something most unusual*—the public downfall and humiliation of popular clergy due to immorality. The media has had a heyday with this. Unfortunately, society often lumps all members of the same profession together. Like other maligned professionals, the clergy has become the object of public scrutiny and ridicule.

*Second, this is a fulfillment of biblical prophecy.* Because false prophets have arisen in the last days, and because many are making merchandise of the gospel—as the Bible said they would—a crisis of confidence has arisen concerning the ministry. Since many people no longer have confidence in the messengers, they disregard all messages. This is great error on their part and dangerous for the welfare of their soul.

In 1 Kings 19, Elijah the prophet made a serious error in judgment. He believed he was the only one who was faithfully serving God and proclaiming the truth. God rebuked him sternly and told him He had seven thousand people in Israel who had never bowed a knee to Baal (v. 18). God also told Elijah that he was not indispensable and that He had someone to take Elijah's place when he was gone, and He had a king waiting to replace Ahab (vv. 16-17).

The lesson is plain. Though some may fall to error and sin, there are many faithful servants of the Lord who preach the truth Sunday after Sunday. Because God has called them and given them the task of preaching the message of life, we should listen to what they say.

This hour desperately needs the anointed preaching of the Word by consecrated vessels. Preaching the whole counsel of God will bring revival to an apostate church and bring conviction upon the unsaved listeners. Faith has to come by hearing, and hearing must come by the Word of God (Rom. 10:17).

A minister of my acquaintance tells of a time he was visited by a certain parishioner who had been attending the minister's church for several months. The person began to ask in all sincerity if the minister was involved with any law enforcement agency or was a private investigator of any sort. The person was very nervous and explained to the pastor that because of his preaching of the Word about sins of dishonesty and unethical behavior, he had come under conviction for wrongs he had committed. He sincerely thought the clergyman might be privy to some secret information about his sins. When the pastor explained to him that his only source of information was the Bible and what it says about sin, the realization that God was watching gripped the man's heart and he repented and experienced a transformation. There is enormous power in anointed preaching!

## Powerful Weapon

Preaching can be a weapon of great importance in spiritual warfare. Anointed preaching is instructional to the believer, comforting to the downtrodden, encouraging to those in despair, inspiring to those who need leadership, and convicting to those guilty of sin. It can also shake the foundations of hell and send a trembling through demonic ranks. When Jesus preached, demons cried out in protest, "What have we to do with thee, thou Jesus of Nazareth?" (Mark 1:24). Powerful preaching has always made the devil nervous, and the reason is simple: the sword of the Spirit cuts and tears down the trouble Satan has built in human lives.

The greatest failure the church could ever suffer would be to stop preaching the gospel. There are those who try to minimize preaching with phrases like "It's not that important in overall ministry," or "You have to do more than just be able to preach." While it is true that a preacher often has a diversity of tasks to perform, these verbal attacks on preaching try to minimize the importance of the preached Word of God. Such critics should examine themselves and ask God to forgive them for minimizing the method He chose to save the world.

When the translators of the King James Version of the Bible wrote their famous preface and addressed it to King James, they made a statement that is noteworthy for us today:

> But among all our joys, there was no one that more filled our hearts, than the blessed continuance of the preaching of God's sacred Word among us; which is the inestimable treasure, which excelleth all the riches of the earth; because the fruit thereof extendeth itself, not only to the time spent in their transitory world, but directeth and disposeth man unto that eternal happiness which is above in heaven.

What a statement of beauty and purpose concerning the preaching of God's Word! These dedicated translators of the Scripture sincerely felt there was no treasure that could be given a nation more valuable than the continuance of the preaching of God's Word. They said this treasure was "inestimable."

A revival of anointed Bible preaching is needed in these last days. Abraham Lincoln said, "When I see a man preach, I like to see him preach as if he were fighting bees!" The great emancipator wanted his preaching seasoned with fiery fervor and godly zeal.

When Paul stood on trial, in one of a series of trials that would eventually lead to his martyrdom, he made a statement that should be every anointed preacher's statement of determination regardless of how the rest of the world feels. In his second letter to Timothy, he told his young protégé this stirring truth:

> At my first answer no man stood with me, but all men forsook me: I pray God that it may not be laid to their charge. Notwithstanding the Lord stood with me, and strengthened me; that by me the preaching might be fully known, and that all the Gentiles might hear: and I was delivered out of the mouth of the lion. And the Lord shall deliver me from every

evil work, and will preserve me unto his heavenly kingdom: to whom be glory for ever and ever. Amen (4:16-18).

Jesus Christ himself was the greatest example of divinely empowered preaching. Luke records the account of Jesus' visit to His hometown of Nazareth in the early years of His earthly ministry. He went into the synagogue on the Sabbath day, as His custom was, and stood up to read from the scroll of Isaiah. Jesus proclaimed, "The Spirit of the Lord is upon Me, because He has anointed Me to preach the gospel to the poor; He has sent Me to heal the brokenhearted, to proclaim liberty to the captives and recovery of sight to the blind, to set at liberty those who are oppressed; to proclaim the acceptable year of the Lord" (Luke 4:18-19 NKJV).

In these verses Jesus attests to being anointed to preach three great truths: (1) the gospel to the poor, (2) liberty to the captives, and (3) the acceptable year of the Lord. Here we have the *message*, the *mission*, and the *messianic time*, all to be preached under divine empowerment by the Lord himself.

Jesus emphatically proclaims to His Nazareth listeners that He is anointed to say what He must say. The word translated as "anointed" (Hebrew, *mashach*; in the Greek, *chrio*), literally means "to smear on with oil as in the consecration of an office or religious service." It is the same word used for *anointing* in 1 Samuel 16:13 when Samuel anointed David to be the king of Israel. It is the same word God used in 1 Kings 19:16 when He commanded Elijah to anoint Elisha to be prophet in Elijah's stead. It is used in John 9:6 when Jesus anointed the eyes of the blind man with clay He had made with dirt and His own spittle. The word means to smear on, cover, spread, and saturate in such a way that there can be no doubt the anointed one has been anointed.

The anointing of the Spirit that Jesus refers to in Luke 4:18 is just that—it is an anointing that requires a literal touch, easily seen and understood. You most assuredly know when it is there, and you know when it is not there. David is the lowly shepherd with the swarthiness and smell of the fold upon him prior to his anointing; but afterward he slays giants and thousands of the enemies of Israel along the way to becoming Israel's greatest king. Elisha is absorbed with his skills as a plowman of oxen until his anointing when he becomes the miracle-working prophet who, even after death, has power in his bones. The blind man in John 9, whose eyes were anointed by Jesus with clay and then told to go wash in the Pool of Siloam, would utter some of the most powerful words in the New Testament when scrutinized by the Pharisees, who told him that Jesus was a sinner. Listen to his "sermon" that has shaken the ages with its forever timely truth: "Whether He is a sinner or not I do not know. One thing I know: that though I was blind, now I see" (John 9:25 NKJV).

The anointing of the Spirit of God continually empowered the ministry and preaching of Jesus, and this pattern flowed like a stream of oil throughout all the narratives of the New Testament and testified to its necessity in the Epistles.

## An Enabling Divine Force

The Bible speaks clearly on the anointing and the supernatural work it does in the lives of men and women. It is more than divine approval, though it is certainly that; it is an enabling force of divine power that takes the person receiving it beyond his or her natural abilities. It then collectively blesses the people of God as a result of its being bestowed in many different ways. Let us examine what the Scripture teaches about how the anointing works.

### The Anointing Works to Unify

In Psalm 133:1-2 we read, "Behold, how good and how pleasant it is for brethren to dwell together in unity! It is like the precious oil upon the head, running down on the beard, the beard of Aaron, running down on the edge of his garments" (NKJV).

The unity of God's people is precious to Him. This passage compares this precious unity to Aaron's anointing. Aaron, the brother of Moses, was Israel's first high priest. He and his sons and descendants were anointed and set aside by God for the service of the priesthood. They served as the go-between for God and the people. All people needed to come to God for redemption. God's law had anointed the priest for this function, and this brought the people to a point of commonality.

The anointing oil that saturated Aaron's head and beard and garments was God's favor upon His own plan of redemption through a high priest. When the Great High Priest, Jesus Christ, announced in the synagogue of Nazareth that the "Spirit of the Lord is upon Me, and He has anointed Me," we have an announcement of unity for God's people. For all of us to come before Him for our redemption is our rallying point of unity. This is the unity of the body of Christ given to us by the anointed Redeemer that destroys division and schism among us.

## The Anointing Breaks the Yoke

In Isaiah 10:27 we read, "The yoke shall be destroyed because of the anointing." Here God promises to give Israel freedom from their Assyrian oppressors. Israel is compared to beasts of burden who slave as an ox under a yoke placed there by its master. However, in the day of their liberation, their freedom comes not as a result of military prowess but because of divine intervention, the anointing of God.

Isaiah said the yoke would be "destroyed." Many would be satisfied with the yoke merely being taken off and set aside. The problem is that such a yoke set aside can be taken up and placed upon the person again. So it is with people who decide to live righteously through the power of fleshly reformation. They give up bad habits and lifestyles, but the yoke is ever in sight and often they find themselves once more in its enslavement. But Isaiah says "the anointing" *destroys* the yoke. The Hebrew word for "destroyed" here is *chabal*, which means "to ruin the yoke, to render it useless, to destroy the threat of the yoke's power." Oh, what the anointing of God can do to those things that once bound us! Anointed preaching of the gospel of Jesus Christ destroys yokes of bondage, fear, and sin.

## The Anointing Assures Us of God's Sovereignty in Our Lives

In 2 Chronicles 20, we see how the people of Moab, Ammon, and Mount Seir came as a multitude to destroy King Jehoshaphat and the people of Israel. Hopelessly outnumbered, with death and destruction seeming imminent, we see the anointing of God fall upon an obscure Israelite named Jahaziel, a Levite of the sons of Asaph. His anointed utterance has several facets of exhortation from God to the people. In verse 15, Jahaziel tells them to not be "afraid nor dismayed" about the size of the enemy, "for the battle is not yours, but God's" (NKJV). In verse 16 they are told to unify themselves. In verse 17, God tells them, through the anointing on Jahaziel, that they don't even have to fight—they need only to "stand still and see the salvation of the Lord" (NKJV).

Ultimately the story ends with the enemies of Israel annihilating each other, and Israel is left to collect bounty and riches. God's anointing and presence turned their trembling hearts of fear into a solid wall of faith. Their standing still in obedience to God not only confused the foe, but it allowed Israel to know there is great reward for heeding a word from God.

Our tendency is to act, often irrationally, and therein is our weakness. How many times does the Bible admonish us to "wait on the Lord"? The value of the assurance brought on by standing still and trusting Him cannot be overestimated. God used an anointed, obscure Levite to remind Israel of the assuring fact that God wants to fight our battles for us.

## The Anointing Purifies

Isaiah the prophet had a vision in the year King Uzziah died. Isaiah saw the Lord "sitting upon a throne, high and lifted up"

(6:1). The seraphim never cease to sing His praises, and the place of the vision itself was shaken and filled with smoke (vv. 3-4). Isaiah's vision of God's holiness and purity reminded him quickly of his own utter uncleanness and impurity. He cries in his woe of his unclean state and understands readily the impurity of his own lips (v. 5). We might imagine the anxiety we would feel as we, the impure, stand before Him who is totally holy and without blemish.

At this moment of Isaiah's profound cries of uncleanness, one of the seraphim leaves the sphere of praise and takes a coal from off the altar and touches Isaiah's lips. Hear the sacred words of the seraphim to Isaiah: "Behold, this has touched your lips; your iniquity is taken away, and your sin purged" (v. 7 NKJV).

Fire has often been used in the Bible as a symbol of God's anointing. From Moses' burning bush in the wilderness of Midian to Elijah's fiery altar atop Mount Carmel, the anointing of God's fire purges and burns out the dross of impurity. The heat of God's holiness allows no vile thing, place, or position in its presence. Isaiah's impurity was that of all people—unclean speech, for he lived among a society whose speech was polluted—and he saw the truth about himself in the anointed presence of God. The anointing does that!

**The Anointing Will Always Promote and Exemplify Christ**

John's vision of Christ in Revelation is an anointed book about an anointed Lord. "His eyes were as a flame of fire; and his feet like unto fine brass, as if they burned in a furnace; . . . and his countenance was as the sun shineth in his strength" (1:14-16).

Paul, in writing to the Romans, boasts not of himself, but instead acknowledges he is a "debtor" to all people everywhere and is "ready to preach the gospel to you that are at Rome also" (1:14-15). To the Corinthians, Paul explicitly states his preaching was "in the power of God" (see 1 Cor. 2:4-5) and predicates this statement by telling them that his only subject matter was "Jesus

Christ, and him crucified" (v. 2). He tells the Galatians, "God forbid that I should boast except in the cross of our Lord Jesus Christ, by whom the world has been crucified to me, and I to the world" (6:14 NKJV). To the young man Timothy he says, "This is a faithful saying and worthy of all acceptance, that Christ Jesus came into the world to save sinners, of whom I am chief" (1 Tim. 1:15 NKJV).

The writer of Hebrews, that anointed book of faith, has the steady theme running through it like a river of refreshing hope, "Christ is better than . . ." He's better than earthly high priests, better than prophets, better than angels, better than the patriarchs, and better than anything the human heart can conceive.

The anointing of God exalts Christ, and Jesus said it best: "And I, if I be lifted up from the earth, will draw all men unto me" (John 12:32).

# 2

# Spirit-Filled Preaching Is Christ-Centered

### J. David Stephens

*For I determined not to know anything among you except Jesus Christ and Him crucified* (1 Cor. 2:2).

The old saying "The more things change, the more they remain the same" may have application to some earlier time in our society, but in the face of today's realities, it is completely irrelevant. Nothing appears to be stable. Changes are occurring so rapidly in every area of culture—population, morality, entertainment, environment, politics, religion, family, and so forth—that many individuals are developing acute psychological trauma. Many of the mental problems, emotional dysfunctions, broken relationships, and an enormous increase in the rate and number of suicides are attributed to these changes. Society seems to be coming unglued at the seams.

These are symptoms of a hurting, wounded world. They are, in fact, indications of the hurt that people have in their souls. Innumerable books have been written that attempt to deal with some of these societal problems. They deal with loneliness, depression, sexual hang-ups, marital dissolutions, mental illness, crime, war, addictions, religious radicalism, and literally scores of other illnesses and ailments afflicting humanity today. Some believers are tempted to throw up their hands and just quit! What is the answer?

*Scriptures are from the New King James Version unless otherwise indicated.

The answers to these afflictions are found in God's unchanging Word. The answer is found most effectively when the Word of God is preached by men and women under the fire and anointing of the Holy Spirit directing the hearer's attention to the risen, victorious, healing, saving, never-changing, soon-coming King—Jesus Christ.

The written Word of the Lord leads us to the living Lord of the Word. And, our attitude toward Him is effectively our choice for eternal life or death. Scripture is replete with instances where men and women of God, under the anointing of the Holy Spirit, preached salvation, healing, deliverance, and direction for lives, pointing the way to Jesus Christ.

Throughout the Book of Acts, the deeds and words of Stephen, Philip, Barnabas, Agabus, Paul, and many other Spirit-anointed preachers lifted a unified voice in exalting the name of their Lord and Master, Jesus Christ. The clear mantra of Paul resonates as the *carpe diem* for the church: "For I determined not to know anything among you except Jesus Christ and Him crucified" (1 Cor. 2:2).

Yet, in recent decades, preaching has devolved into group therapy as pastors presented series on financial management, marriage dynamics, relational "how-tos," and a myriad of social ills. Many now preach from a "gathered idea" and find scriptures to be proof texts for their claims, principles, and the subject *du jour* in society. There is a tendency that has drifted into Pentecostal circles of finding a good book and preaching through its chapters, or parroting the latest video marvel posted online. This kind of preaching—the kind that lacks freshness of relationship with Jesus and is minus the toil of discipleship and repentance—never captures the essence of what preaching is meant to be. For this reason, those who are biblical proponents and believers in the wholeness of God's activity in the world must pay careful attention to keep Jesus at the center of their preaching.

It is ironic that many believe Pentecostal preaching is Spirit-centered, or centered on spiritual gifts. The truth is that Spirit-anointed preaching will always point to the work of Jesus Christ. After all, the fullest expression of Pentecost is the witness of Jesus Christ—just read the Book of Acts! The inaugural sermon of Pentecostal preaching was a full-gospel message centering on Jesus Christ. On the Day of Pentecost, inspired by the Holy Spirit, Peter authoritatively asserted: "Therefore let all Israel be assured of this: God has made this Jesus, whom you crucified, both Lord and Christ. . . . Repent, and be baptized, every one of you, in the name of Jesus Christ for the forgiveness of your sins. And you will receive the gift of the Holy Spirit" (Acts 2:36-38 NIV).

## Christ-Centered Preaching Calls for a Christ-Centered Preacher

Today, in a market of ideas, people tend to pick and choose what to believe and how to practice that belief. The centrality of Jesus in preaching should be directing, leading, coaching, and inspiring people to love, embrace, forgive, accept, touch, and be with humanity as Jesus was. Preaching Jesus produces "Jesus-ness."

If Jesus is preached as the center of life and practice, a personality of Jesus will emerge in the church. Many pastors say they see self-centered, tight-fisted, unforgiving, and unloving people populating the pews and chairs of our gathering spaces. Why is that? It could be because the paradigm of teaching is centered on *felt needs* of individuals and they have become seekers of *better lives*—that is, more comfort, less demand—and they want those "better lives" right now. Very often, churches are not producing communities of servants, and that is the most telling metric in the evaluation of preaching and discipleship endeavors.

"Does it matter if it's real?" These words (in bold text) caught my attention as I scanned the front cover of *USA Today* (Jan. 25,

2013). The question referenced several public issues that are not what they appear to be. These included reality-TV shows that are "staged," sports heroes taking performance-enhancing drugs, and a superstar vocalist who used a "voice-over" at a major event that was broadcast throughout the world. The article asked if the American public knows or cares that they are constantly being deceived. One of those interviewed was the founding CEO and president of the Association of Certified Fraud Examiners. He was clear in saying that the public is very aware of the deception, and they feel betrayed.

This feeling of being deceived is pervasive. It presents a huge challenge for the church. Unfortunately, many have concluded that church services are practically the same as reality-TV shows and staged reenactments. By and large, Americans believe God is real but doubt the spiritual authority vested in the church. The sad truth is that in many cases the church advertises more than it delivers and comes across sounding prerecorded—not live!

There is a mandate for authenticity. This should remind the church of the response Jesus gave to a question asked two thousand years ago. Some Jews were tagging along in the crowd following Jesus. Intrigued by the miracles He performed, they desired the power to become miracle workers themselves. When the opportunity presented itself, they asked Him, "What shall we do, that we may work the works of God?" His answer was short and direct: "This is the work of God, that you believe in Him whom He sent" (John 6:28-29). What did He mean? He meant that "believing" on Jesus activates ministry in one's life! While this seems simplistic, it is actually profound. Doing good things is not necessarily the same as doing God's work.

The issue facing the church today is not whether God is real, but whether or not the church is real. Often, it seems that Pentecostals are asking God, "Move among us. . . . Come down into our midst and show Yourself strong. . . . Do mighty works among us." At times, others pray something like this: "O God, be real in me!" It may be that He wants the church to start praying, "O God, show me how I can be real in Jesus Christ!"

Preaching—standing before dozens, hundreds, or thousands weekly and speaking about God, for God, and from God—is a sacred trust. Jesus-centeredness in the church begins with the leader being "lorded" by Jesus. If that is not a reality, then no amount of preaching the right text will have lasting fruitfulness. Why? Only the preacher who believes to the point of being a genuine Christ-follower can effectively proclaim Christ as Lord.

## Why Is Christ-Centered Pentecostal Preaching Important?

Preaching is a catalyst, but refinement is a process. Ministry is holistic: it seeks to impact individuals *spiritually* in their will, *emotionally* in their decisions, and *physically* through their activity. Preaching is only one part of that, but get preaching wrong and it all goes wrong! As disciples, believers must be immersed in the life and way of Jesus so they can teach how He is Lord of our lives and how His mandates govern our actions and reactions in every arena of life. Every believer should be asking . . .

How is Jesus Lord of my stewardship?

How is Jesus Lord of my relationships?

How is Jesus Lord of my work?

How is Jesus Lord of my time?

In this sense, all Pentecostal sermons intersect the new spiritual realities in the believer's life in Christ. The significance of one's life in Christ should be proclaimed in the power of the Holy Spirit, inasmuch as the Spirit makes the new aspects of life in Christ living realities.

The turn of the twentieth century saw intellectual results from the Age of Enlightenment to the modern period. The modern period was marked by intellectualism that assumed all truth could be objectively known. In theological circles, scholars believed they could decipher the history of biblical stories and eliminate all references to the supernatural, or acts of God. The modern period was distinguished by a rational arrogance that everything could be scientifically analyzed and man could speak authoritatively about everything in the universe. The world revolved around intellectual mankind. From their perspective, there was no need for God—humanity would continue to evolve in its understanding and problem-solving. Then, philosophers began to question not only the "rational" and logical conclusions but also some of the premises that were assumed to be true.

These philosophers were the fathers of the "postmodern" period. Their approach to understanding the universe invaded all the sciences and liberal arts and found a fertile place for growth in the college classrooms of educators in the Western Hemisphere. This skepticism meant there was a possibility of multiple explanations and understandings of the universe. There were no absolutes. Additionally, with no absolutes, tolerance of various life-views was necessary.

The new skepticism is suspicious of authoritative figures speaking with confidence about any absolute truths. Instead, the new skeptics value authentic voices that recognize the bounds of their knowledge and express a humility that will embrace multiple viewpoints, even if they are contrary to the one being proclaimed. One response by some younger Evangelicals to this new postmodernism is the "emergent church." The leaders of the emergent church are generally selective in adopting those parts of theology from various theological and denominational perspectives that are acceptable to the postmodern thinker. Preaching is not to be "against" anything or too confident in its expression. Tolerance of competing worldviews is acceptable.

This postmodern age desperately needs effective Spirit-filled proclamation that demonstrates a true humility and clings to biblical authenticity. Christ-centered, Spirit-filled preaching can provide the answer for this age.

The culture of the New Testament included multiple worldviews and theological perspectives vying for acceptance by the masses. A common language and monetary system made the known world in the New Testament far more connected than in any earlier period of history.

Postmodern culture is similarly connected by the language of technology. News from around the globe is learned in minutes from the time it happens. Media outlets give commentary to explain cultural and historical differences. This enables a more complete understanding of the rest of the world. Knowledge of a subject no longer requires travel to a university so one can sit and study. Today, simply click a few buttons and intricate complexities are explained to anyone who can read. So, the postmodern period has many of the same contextual aspects of the first-century New Testament period. In that time, God supplied His answer through the power of the Holy Spirit—Jesus Christ.

Jesus Christ is the authentic expression of the Creator. He is truth. Now, preaching must distinguish between the limited human explanation of the Christ and the person of Jesus Christ. He is revealed in Scripture and is the ultimate, absolute, inexhaustible truth. In fact, there is no truth, no authenticity, outside of Jesus Christ. He is the full expression of the God who creates meaning and life.

## What Does Christ-Centered Preaching Look Like?

While not every sermon will mention some part of the narrative of the life and ministry of Jesus Christ, He should at least be the backdrop of every sermon. Old Testament passages cannot be understood without viewing them through the lenses of the reality that God sent Jesus Christ to reconcile the world to Him. Every New Testament blessing or truth is within the redemptive context of the work of the Atonement provided by Jesus Christ. In this way, all sermons, all roads, pass by the Cross.

Like the disciples learned on the road to Emmaus, all Scripture is fulfilled in Jesus Christ, and the preacher's task is to explain how that is so. Since believers are new creatures in Christ, how does a particular passage relate to the believer?

Whether the passage refers to the challenge of discipleship, the blessing of healing, or any other spiritual matter, it applies within the context of one redeemed in Christ.

The Holy Spirit does not come to speak of Himself; He comes to testify of Jesus Christ, to make known all things that Jesus taught to His disciples (John 16:13-14). Accordingly, a Spirit-inspired sermon cannot and will not focus on the believer or the preacher—his or her spirituality or demonstration of power. Unfortunately, one can find many examples of sermons preached by Pentecostal preachers where the sermon testifies of the attributes of the preacher in the attempt to gain admiration. This is the model of preaching of one who is trying to build up a ministry and a crowd to follow it. The Holy Spirit instead lifts up Jesus Christ.

The Holy Spirit intends to build only the kingdom of God in Jesus Christ, not a human ministry or a crowd for human adulation. If the Holy Spirit has the singular purpose to exalt Jesus Christ and if He inspires Pentecostal preaching, how can Spirit-empowered preaching testify to anything else?

After Jesus was tempted by Satan in the wilderness, He entered the synagogue in His hometown and read from Isaiah: "The Spirit of the Lord is upon Me, because He has anointed Me to preach . . ." (Luke 4:18-19). The Spirit-inspired preaching of Jesus brought healing to the blind, deliverance to captives, and the declaring of the year of salvation. If the Spirit-inspired preaching of Jesus is outlined by proclaiming healing, deliverance, and salvation, then Pentecostal preaching in the power of the Holy Spirit will be similarly formed. Can there be a more important proclamation than how Jesus brings salvation, healing, and deliverance to a broken world?

In Christ, there is truth in love. As believers are confronted with their utter humanity and failings, when they call upon Jesus they also find the answer—His grace and redemption—to those failings. Many postmodern thinkers believe Christ is *one* way, but they need to confront the reality of the Christ who is the *only* way. Spirit-filled preaching will proclaim the truth of Christ—both in setting forth the need for redemption and the answer to that need in the person of Jesus Christ.

## Christ-Centered Preaching Delivers Hope

Although it may not be noticeable on their faces, a large number of people in our congregations struggle with a deep-seated sense of *worthlessness* and *hopelessness*. Being first cousins, both feelings are vexations resulting from humanity's sinful condition and are usually only attended to cosmetically. Some bandage them with the procurement of things—electronic gadgets, clothing, cars, and other possessions. Others engage in a more destructive form of "self-medicating" by attacking other people. "Hurting" people hurt other people.

Sometimes the intellectual elite stumble onto truth concerning humanity's spiritual condition that Pentecostals found in Scripture long ago. One such discovery was made by an ardent rival of Christianity about one hundred years ago. Sigmund Freud asserted that the sense of guilt was "the most important problem in the development of civilization . . . the price we pay for our advance in civilization is a loss of happiness through the heightening of the sense of guilt."[1] For him, the guilty conscience is the result of belonging to a civilized society that advocates ethical and moral judgments, and guilt lies deep in the unconscious. It manifests in anxiety and discontent, according to Freud, which became the hypothesis for Freudian psychology. He sought to release his patient from guilt by attempting to diminish its substance and designating it as just another psychological phenomenon.

Fast-forward to today. Guilt continues to drive discontent, a sense of worthlessness, and hopelessness in the twenty-first century. Postmodern skeptics offer no hope, because there is nothing upon which they can depend—nothing is absolute. Modern optimism about the ability of human intellectualism has fallen short—so-called critical thinkers recognize the empty and unfulfilled hopes in human rationality.

The absolute truth is that unregenerate humanity stands in its sinful condition guilty before a holy God, but through divine intervention, Jesus Christ now stands in humanity's place. Christ took our sins to the cross, convening His righteousness with the required sacrifice of atonement. Christ's righteousness is humanity's hope! Faith in Christ and His provision for us on the cross is the remedy for our sinfulness.

Pentecostal preaching delivers hope in the proclamation of Christ's victory over sin and the wiles of the devil. It is good to remember that Satan roams about as a "roaring lion, seeking whom he may devour" (1 Peter 5:8), but he is powerless when we place our hope and faith in Christ. God's eyes are over the righteous, and His ears are attentive to their cries. After all, we are His crowning achievement, created in His image and likeness. Many have become fallen prey because they do not know their position of victory in Christ Jesus. The church is the place for hearing Pentecostal preaching that raises the hope of overcoming power promised to every child of God. Believers need to be constantly reminded that "God shall supply all [their] need according to His riches in glory by Christ Jesus" (Phil. 4:19). Followers of Christ need to hear faith-building messages assuring them they can do "all things through Christ who strengthens [them]" (v. 13).

Pentecostal preaching that is Christ-centered infuses His hope to saints and sinners alike. Regardless of how desperate people have become or how different they are from the rest of our church family, if they are breathing we must preach the hope that Jesus promised to "whosoever will"!

People know when they are not where they need to be spiritually and when they are not doing what they should do. They also know when they are not living the life they should live. They don't have to be reminded every week how awful they are. But they do need to be told there is hope for them. In every sermon, ministers must be intentional and persuasive in presenting the anointed truth of God—that in Christ, we all have *hope*!

Therefore, in today's searching and hurting world, let the church pray fervently that Pentecostal preaching will be modeled after the Christ-centered preaching of the New Testament. May every Pentecostal preacher come to understand these facts: (1) a Christ-centered preacher will always preach a Christ-centered message, (2) why this is so important in these last days, and (3) what Christ-centered preaching looks like. This is the message of hope that will bring salvation to the world.

# 3

# Spirit-Filled Preaching Is a Word From the Lord

### Wallace J. Sibley

*Then I said, "I will not make mention of Him, nor speak anymore in His name." But His word was in my heart like a burning fire shut up in my bones; I was weary of holding it back, and I could not* (Jer. 20:9).

Many books have been written about the Spirit-filled life, and much has been gleaned from them. The titles have included *How to Receive the Gift of the Holy Spirit; Who Is the Holy Ghost?; Leading a Spirit-Filled Life; Encountering the Holy Spirit; What Happens When the Spirit Comes In?; The Person and Work of the Holy Spirit*; and the list goes on and on.

A number of books have particularly focused on the Spirit's role in preaching, including these: *Spirit-Led Preaching*; *Preaching in the Holy Spirit*; and *Demonstrating the Anointing*. This chapter will show that Spirit-filled preaching is a word from the Lord.

Jeremiah 20:9 indicates that Spirit-filled preaching is more than the personal opinion of the preacher. It transcends current events and consists of much more than a few pages gleaned from the Internet. Spirit-filled preaching is a word directly from God . . . an anointed burden God places on an individual . . . a message from God seasoned with grace.

*Scriptures are from the *New King James Version* unless otherwise indicated.

By the time we reach Jeremiah 20, the prophet had obediently proclaimed God's word in the face of much opposition. Even his friends and family had opposed his message. The message, however, was an irresistible force God had placed within his heart. Jeremiah could not refrain from delivering the burden of his soul. God's message was like a "burning fire" that could not be contained. Effective preaching always has its beginnings as a burning fire in the preacher's heart. It is more than just a sermon. Powerful preaching consists of a deep burden that cannot be contained.

The first chapter of Jeremiah shows the young prophet being instructed by God:

> The word of the Lord came to me, saying, "Jeremiah, what do you see"? And I said, "I see a branch of an almond tree." Then the Lord said to me, "You have seen well, for I am ready to perform My word." And the word of the Lord came to me the second time, saying, "What do you see?" And I said, "I see a boiling pot, and it is facing away from the north" (vv. 11-13).

Jeremiah initially resisted the call of God, thinking himself too young for such an important task (v. 6). God, however, promised the young man, "I have put My words in your mouth" (v. 9). Our world needs a generation of Jeremiahs, young men and women who will receive the call of God and hear the word of the Lord when it comes to them. If the gospel is to reach the world and if revival is to break out in America, we must have an army of preachers who go forth with the words of God in their mouths.

The prophet Jonah heard from God and was instructed where he should go and what he should do: "Now the word of the Lord came to Jonah the son of Amittai, saying, 'Arise, go to Nineveh, that great city, and cry out against it; for their wickedness has come up before Me'" (Jonah 1:1-2). Even though Jonah had other ideas and personal opinions, the end results show the Word of God has preeminence. Jonah went to Nineveh and preached the word of the Lord, and the city of Nineveh repented.

## Spirit-Filled Preaching Is a Word From the Lord

To think that Jonah's or Jeremiah's ingenuity, wisdom, or skill could accomplish their powerful ministries would be a mistake. Their power came through their anointing by the Holy Spirit.

Read with me from the pages of Ezekiel's prophecies:

> The hand of the Lord came upon me and brought me out in the Spirit of the Lord, and set me down in the midst of the valley; and it was full of bones. Then He caused me to pass by them all around, and behold, there were very many in the open valley; and indeed they were very dry. And He said to me, "Son of man, can these bones live?" So I answered, "O Lord God, You know." Again He said to me, "Prophesy to these bones, and say to them, 'O dry bones, hear the word of the Lord!'" (37:1-4).

Israel is symbolized here under the figure of a valley of dry bones, being brought back to life in the bodies of a great army of men. Even now the Word of God is yet being fulfilled with many Jewish descendants returning to Israel. (The Church of God is playing a major role in this with our "Ministry to Israel.")

In Ezekiel 38, again we see and hear God speaking to the prophet. As God spoke to him, Ezekiel in turn spoke to the people and could rightly say: "Thus says the Lord."

> Now the word of the Lord came to me, saying, "Son of man, set your face against Gog, of the land of Magog, the prince of Rosh, Meshech, and Tubal, and prophesy against him, and say, 'Thus says the Lord God: "Behold, I am against you, O Gog, the prince of Rosh, Meshech, and Tubal. I will turn you around, put hooks into your jaws, and lead you out, with all your army, horses, and horsemen, all splendidly clothed, a great company with bucklers and shields, all of them handling swords. Persia, Ethiopia, and Libya are with them, all of them with shield and helmet; Gomer and all its troops; the house of Togarmah from the far north and all its troops—many people are with you. Prepare yourself and be ready, you and all your companies that are gathered about you; and be a guard for them"'" (vv. 1-7).

## Pentecostal Preaching Moves People to Action

After Jesus ascended to heaven, the disciples began a prayer meeting that lasted ten days. About 120 men and women waited and prayed for the promise of Jesus: "Behold, I send the Promise of My Father upon you; but tarry in the city of Jerusalem until you are endued with power from on high" (Luke 24:49).

As the believers were praying in the Upper Room, "suddenly" there was a sound of a great windstorm in the skies above them, "and it filled the whole house where they were sitting" (Acts 2:2). Then, what looked like flames of fire appeared and settled on their heads. And everyone present was filled with the Holy Spirit and began speaking in languages they did not know, for the Spirit gave them this ability. The disciples were not theologically trained, but the Holy Spirit and the anointing made the difference. "Many wonders and signs were done through the apostles. . . . And the Lord added to the church daily those who were being saved" (vv. 43, 47). "When [the Jewish leaders] saw the boldness of Peter and John, and perceived that they were uneducated and untrained men, they marveled. And they realized that they had been with Jesus" (4:13).

It seems as if the church is moving away from being led by the Holy Spirit, or even being moved by the Spirit. Too much effort today is directed by human plans, programs, and opinions instead of trusting God's Word to accomplish the work of God. I hunger to see the day when we allow the Holy Spirit to take full control of every situation. It feels good, it sounds good, and it is good to say, "It seemed good to the Holy Spirit, and to us . . ." (15:28). Our agenda, plans, programs, and opinions are good and right in their place. But when the Holy Spirit takes over a situation, it's best to take our hands off the steering wheel and yield to the presence of God.

In 1930, a student in the third grade stole a nickel and was suspended from school. The young boy had not learned to read. His mother, a member of the Church of God, would take him with her to church at night because she did not want to walk from church alone. He received salvation and was filled with the Holy Spirit as a teenager. God called the young man to preach.

I heard him preach many times. He usually spent about ten minutes collecting his thoughts and calming his nerves before attempting to read his Scripture text. After he presented the Scripture text and began to preach, the congregation could feel and visualize heaven as a heavy anointing coming over him. Many along with me in the audience felt that anointing. Those who did not know him well never suspected that he could not read. He served the church for many years as administrative bishop before he went to be with the Lord.

Ask anyone who knew him what they would say about his preaching. Their answer would be, "His preaching moved me to action." If you were a singer, it would move you to sing better. If you were a Sunday school teacher, it would move you to teach better. If you were a preacher, it would move you to preach better. His anointed preaching would draw the saved closer to a never-failing God.

## Pentecostal Preaching Has a Burden and Conviction

When the Word of God is preached effectively, the minister speaks what the Word says and the way it should be understood, not giving the minister's personal interpretation. The preacher emphasizes what is written and what is meant by what is written. However, the way the Word is delivered could make the difference in the way it is received or rejected by the congregation. Some methods of delivery are cold, conceited, closed-minded, without interest or the ability to relate or influence. However, there is a mode of delivery that brings interest, challenges, motivates, and, most of all, produces a desire to embrace change. It inspires the hearers to receive the Word while creating an inspirational atmosphere for positive outcomes in their lives.

## Pentecostal Preaching Is Inspired by the Holy Spirit

Spirit-filled preaching trumps human wisdom or enticing words, and is delivered through the Holy Spirit. Paul declared, "My speech and my preaching were not with persuasive words of human wisdom, but in demonstration of the Spirit and of power" (1 Cor. 2:4). The apostle Paul did not resort to the arts and enticements of Greek oratory or philosophy, but he instead depended on the demonstration of the Holy Spirit and power. He reminded his audience of all the teachings he had received from institutions of higher learning; however, his dependence was totally on the Holy Spirit.

Motivational speaker Dale Carnegie said, "Your purpose is to make your audience see what you see, hear what you hear, and feel what you feel. Relevant detail couched in concrete colorful language is the best way to re-create the incident as it happened and to picture it for the audience."[1] Speaking now in spiritual terms, I have heard it said that the minister must assist the audience to see things that are hidden from them. The Lord makes it clear when He tells His disciples, "To you it has been given to know the mystery of the kingdom of God" (Mark 4:11).

The minister must allow the Holy Spirit to exhibit wisdom that gives genuine understanding of the Word of God. The preacher should strive to be invisible—seeking to express, not impress. When the minister becomes concerned with being the center of attraction rather than allowing the Holy Spirit to be manifest in the preaching, the essence of what the Spirit is providing through the Word will lose its focus. The Word must take precedence and be the center of attention. Paul wanted to make sure the preached Word by the Holy Spirit was the focus of attraction. By presenting himself as the mere human he was, his dependence was on the Holy Spirit and not on his human abilities.

One Sunday morning, the mayor of our city walked into my church unannounced. I had already given my text and subject and could not call my music team up to do another number. I was, to say the least, grossly intimidated. As I preached, however, the Holy Spirit touched me, the anointing took over, and I preached with great boldness. Afterward, I told my wife, Dorothy, that I wished the president of the United States had been there!

## Pentecostal Preaching Empowers for Service

Holy Spirit preaching provides empowerment to the listeners. The apostle Paul ministered "by the word of truth, by the power of God" (2 Cor. 6:7), "in demonstration of the Spirit and of power, that [his hearers'] faith should not be in the wisdom of men but in the power of God" (1 Cor. 2:4-5). Thus, he reminded them to depend on the Holy Spirit and not on human wisdom.

Throughout 1 Corinthians 2, Paul reminds the readers that Holy Spirit preaching is inspired by God and reveals the wisdom of the Spirit. He reminds them their faith should be the fulfillment of what the Spirit brings when the minister is anointed by the Holy Spirit. This empowerment provides the opportunity for God to perform miracles, to illuminate the Scriptures, and to give clarity—to clear the way for salvation. Most of all, the Holy Spirit empowers the believers to trust God and allow them to gain a deeper trust in God to answer prayer.

After fifty years of gospel preaching, I am still amazed at what Holy Spirit preaching brings to a service. In preparing a message, one usually wonders how the sermon will flow or conclude. Once, I was preaching during a community service, following the manuscript outline, and waiting for the Holy Spirit anointing. In the middle of the sermon, both the speaker and the audience knew things were happening that were greater than the preacher, the audience, and the church. God changed the atmosphere and moved the service into a different direction. People in the congregation began to weep uncontrollably. Others fell prostrate with their faces on the floor crying out to God. All were moved by the anointed preaching. Spontaneous healings were celebrated, confessions of past sins were shared, apologies were given, and spiritual healings took place. It was God the

Holy Spirit at work, taking a normal service and turning it into a powerful move for His glory.

I have held several weddings at the conclusion of revivals because, during the revival, couples were convicted of living together without being married. I have seen men go back to their wives, and women go back to their husbands, after hearing the preached Word. Many marriages have been restored and families united when the anointed Word has been delivered.

Spirit-filled preaching causes the minister to become invisible and allows the Holy Spirit to present Christ as the answer to any challenging situation. Holy Spirit preaching confirms and demonstrates to the audience that they are more than conquerors through Christ. The Holy Spirit gives us the ability to find resources within God's Word and provides us the faith to succeed. Preaching in the Spirit lifts the audience to a level of faith that allows God to conquer their fears, disappointments, and negative challenges and releases in them the ability to triumph over any situation. This type of preaching will empower others to take this Word everywhere: "Therefore those who were scattered went everywhere preaching the word" (Acts 8:4).

- The Holy Spirit is not a novelty; He is a necessity.
- The Holy Spirit is not an extra; He is essential.
- The Holy Spirit is not a convenience; He is a requirement.

David grew up in his father's (Jesse's) house, the youngest of eight brothers. He served as a shepherd, a harpist, a psalmist, a warrior, and a king. Along the way, he faced many challenges, from his lowly job as a shepherd to his lofty position as the king. David was referred to as "a man after [God's] own heart" (Acts 13:22). Take note from Psalm 51—when there were challenges in his family, in his kingdom, and in himself, David knew how to stay in fellowship and relationship with God. He prayed, "Do not cast me away from Your presence, and do not take Your Holy Spirit from me" (v. 11). King David did as all of us should do— come clean with God. David seems to be saying, "Abuse me and misuse me, but do not take away the Holy Spirit. Detest me or arrest me, but do not take away the Holy Spirit. Take my palace, take my power, but do not take away the Holy Spirit. Take all of my money and my honey, but please do not take away Your Holy Spirit from me."

We need the Holy Spirit for guidance and direction. We need Him to be our Comforter. We need Him for power and authority to be a witness for Jesus Christ. "For as many as are led by the Spirit of God, these are sons of God" (Rom. 8:14).

# 4

# Spirit-Filled Preaching Is Evangelistic

### M. Thomas Propes

*"Repent, and let every one of you be baptized in the name of Jesus Christ for the remission of sins; and you shall receive the gift of the Holy Spirit. For the promise is to you and to your children, and to all who are afar off, as many as the Lord our God will call"* (Acts 2:38).

The first-ever Spirit-filled sermon was evangelistic.

Having received the baptism in the Holy Spirit in the Pentecost-Day outpouring, Peter, standing with his fellow disciples, proclaimed the story of Jesus and called for the questioning multitude to repent and follow Jesus. When Peter gave that first Pentecostal altar call under the anointing of the Holy Spirit, he set the standard for Pentecostal preaching. Whatever other sermons we preach—doctrinal, theological, devotional, instructional, pastoral care—we must first and foremost preach for evangelistic decisions. We must present the claims of Christ in the power of the Holy Spirit, fully expecting unsaved hearers to repent and call on Him for forgiveness. This is the mandate of Christ, made clear in Mark's account of the Great Commission: "Go into all the world and preach the gospel to every creature. He who believes and is baptized will be saved; but he who does not believe will be condemned" (16:15-16).

*Scriptures are from the New King James Version.*

Evangelistic preaching is the hallmark of the New Testament Pentecostal preacher, demonstrated not only by Peter, but also by the apostle Paul. Paul is typically considered the theologian, the teacher, the apologist of the Christian movement; yet his heartbeat was evangelism, as demonstrated by his own testimony. His proclamations include:

- "I am not ashamed of the gospel of Christ, for it is the power of God to salvation for everyone who believes" (Rom. 1:16).
- "For Christ did not send me to baptize, but to preach the gospel, not with wisdom of words, lest the cross of Christ should be made of no effect" (1 Cor. 1:17).
- "For I determined not to know anything among you except Jesus Christ and Him crucified . . . that your faith should not be in the wisdom of men but in the power of God" (2:2, 5).
- "I have become all things to all men, that I might by all means save some" (9:22).

Paul's confrontations with the Philippian jailer (Acts 16), with Agrippa (ch. 26), and with his guards in the Roman prison (ch. 28) evidence his priority calling: winning the lost to Christ through evangelism. It was the calling of the apostles, and it is our calling as well.

## The Challenges of Evangelistic Preaching

*Evangelistic preaching* is "proclaiming the gospel of salvation to men and women in the power of the Holy Spirit with a view to their conversion to Christ and incorporation into His church." It is a definition most agree with, but its practice seems to have fallen into disuse among many. Many of us will remember in past years that rarely a Sunday passed without the pastor confronting his hearers with an altar call. Not so much anymore.

## A Matter of Life or Death

The insistence of Scripture is that preachers are bound to challenge people with the decision to commit themselves to Christ. It is a matter of spiritual life and death. It is an invitation to find abundant life here and now. It results in changed lives, and it ensures that converted people will live eternally in God's presence. It brings deliverance from a sinful lifestyle, a sense of joy because of forgiveness from sin and guilt, and an awareness of a new and purposeful life. It is what God desires for men and women, and it is what hungry-hearted people are crying out for. And the preacher is most often the instrument through whom it happens.

When the Pentecost-Day crowd heard a clear presentation of the gospel message, the Bible says they cried out, asking what they should do. The preacher told them to repent, and informed them about the gift of the Holy Spirit.

I can't tell you of all the people I've seen who stood at their pew during the altar call, more often than not gripping the back of the pew as they resisted God's call; then, upon their surrender, witnessing the joy and rejoicing that comes when they yielded their lives in repentance.

I vividly remember my own father's conversion. After years of "running from the Lord," as the old-timers used to call it, Dad came home one afternoon and announced we were going that very evening to the City Auditorium in Charleston, South Carolina, to hear an evangelist by the name of Oral Roberts. Even as an eight-year-old, I was surprised that Dad wanted to go to that meeting; my mother, however, was overwhelmed.

Somewhere in the midst of Brother Roberts' preaching and multiplied hundreds of people shouting and praising God, my father tapped me on the shoulder and said, "When your Momma stops shouting, tell her I'll be back after a while."

"Yes sir," I replied, "but where are you going?"

He answered, "I'm going to get saved. I can't stand this any longer!" My father's conversion was brought about by the prayers of my precious mother and as a direct result of evangelistic preaching.

The rejoicing that takes place when a new believer is born into the family of God reminds me of a definition of *love* I once heard: "*Love* is an outward inexpressibility of an inward 'all-overish-ness.'" That's the only way to describe the joy of a new convert!

## Making the Gospel Clear

The first Spirit-filled evangelistic message teaches us something about the content of our own soulwinning sermons. The proclamation must be based on Scripture. We're not sure how long Peter preached; we have a manuscript, but it is followed by the statement, "With many other words he testified and exhorted them" (Acts 2:40). However, of the printed portion of the sermon, which contains twenty-five verses, ten of them are direct quotes of biblical verses. Peter's sermon was firmly based on "Thus says the Lord."

Jesus must be at the heart of the message. Peter told his Jerusalem audience, "God has made this Jesus, whom you crucified, both Lord and Christ" (v. 36). He affirmed that Jesus did miracles, wonders, and signs; that He was crucified, and then rose from the dead; and He is worthy of being followed. The invitation centered on Jesus.

A good evangelistic sermon will often include the telling of the gospel events (Jesus came, died, arose); witnessing to the gospel affirmations (the Incarnation and the Atonement); testifying to the gospel promises (forgiveness, peace with God, the Holy Spirit); and making clear the gospel demands (repentance, baptism, changed life).

Theologians call this the *kerygma*, or the "content of the gospel message." It is different from *didaskalia*, the "teaching sermon." Both are vital to Christian growth. Both are part of the

Great Commission ("preaching" and "teaching"). But it begins with the evangelistic pronouncement.

## The Obstacles to Evangelistic Preaching

If evangelistic preaching was easy, everyone would do it. Unfortunately, it is not so.

### The Tenor of the Times

In the eyes of many preachers, it is difficult to preach at all in the twenty-first century. Today's hearers, especially people not associated with the church—and even some within the church—think it is a bit old-fashioned to hold to the idea of a single person standing with moral authority and speaking a truth that demands obedience. The idea is ridiculed by some: "Who is he, thinking he can tell me what to do!"

The younger the audience, the more difficult it may be to communicate the saving gospel to them. By the time they finish high school, they have watched 22,000 hours of television. They have been conditioned to pay attention for five minutes, then take a mental break (time for a commercial), then come back to the main idea. During every 30 minutes or hour they view TV, a situation is introduced, examined, and the problem resolved. The viewers do not have to wrestle with ideas. They do not have to take any action as a result of having invested the time. And then they come into church and are expected to sit for 45 minutes or so, doing something different than they have done all those thousands of hours—listening and mentally following (without benefit of moving pictures!).

Some preachers ignore the reality. A savvy preacher, however, will sprinkle illustrations, a change of cadence in the voice, a bit of humor, or some other attention-relieving device within the sermon in order to give the "mental break" listeners may have been trained to expect. This is not caving in to the devil; it's just using common sense.

The even-younger MTV audiences are more challenging. They have been taught to think in vivid, quick, repeated images that burst on the imagination. How can the pastor compete? Some like to use PowerPoint outlines, movie clips, or homemade videos.

It seems more than we can cope with. But we must not forget that evangelistic preaching is a work for two—the preacher and the Holy Spirit. We must do all the preparation we are capable of doing, and then we must depend on the Holy Spirit to do His part, too. His work is that of conviction, and He is good at it. Despite our limitations and the strength of the challenges we face, He is God. He has no limitations, and He can cause a breakthrough.

## The Opposition of the Audience

What are the expectations of the congregation to whom we deliver the Word?

In many churches, the culture has devalued the authority of the pastor. The people like for the pastor to be the chaplain of their religious expectations and the guardian of their cherished traditions—nothing more . . . certainly not a challenger of their lifestyles!

A recent article on the role of the pastor tells of a group of members talking about their ideal minister. Various ideas were exchanged, until one young man said, "I'm tired of preachers telling me what to believe and do. I think they ought to just make suggestions to us!" Heads shook in agreement around the room, and no one seemed to object. With this sort of thinking, it would be no wonder if the Ten Commandments were to be unveiled in the future as the "Ten Suggestions." Satan puts a veil over the truth, and only the Holy Spirit can penetrate it. "He will convict the world of sin, and of righteousness, and of judgment" (John 16:8).

The preacher needs to weigh the expectations of the congregation against the expectations of the One who called him.

## The Preacher's Own Personality

Every preacher is called to be an evangelist. The verb translated *evangelize* in one of its forms are used more than fifty times in the New Testament, indicating something of its importance. The noun *evangelist* is used only three times. Philip, one of the seven deacons chosen in Acts 6, is identified as an evangelist, and we see him fulfilling his ministry in a citywide crusade in Samaria and in a personal encounter with the Ethiopian eunuch (ch. 8), as well as at home with his own family. His four daughters were recognized as prophets. In Ephesians 4:11, an evangelist is one of the gifted people God places in the Church. In 2 Timothy 4, Paul, at the end of his ministry, is counseling his young protégé about the scope of his future pastoral ministry and tells him, "Preach the word! . . . Do the work of an evangelist" (vv. 2, 5).

In 2 Corinthians 5:18, Paul explains God has committed to us "the ministry of reconciliation." Two verses later, he reveals it is the focus of his own ministry: "We implore you on Christ's behalf, be reconciled to God" (v. 20).

Regardless of the tenor of the times or the opposition of people who do not want to be told what to do, the pastor's calling includes evangelism. We must evangelize. A pastor may say he doesn't feel called to be an evangelist. "My ministry is pastoral, to teach and care for the flock," is a common attitude. "I'll invite an evangelist to come by and preach the revival sermons."

The late Sam Shoemaker, an Episcopalian bishop, summed up the situation this way: "In the Great Commission, the Lord has called us to be—like Peter—fishers of men. We've turned the commission around so that we have become merely keepers of the aquarium."[1]

Richard Stoll Armstrong, in his book *The Pastor as Evangelist,* reaches back for an illustration to the years when Red Skelton was a well-known comedian. In his routine, Skelton would sometimes play the part of Clem Kadiddlehopper, the fearful and reluctant salesman. He would timidly approach someone's front door, knock, and quickly turn away, saying, "No one's home . . . I hope, I hope, I hope."[2] There might be a few pastors whose approach to evangelistic preaching is the same.

*Preach the Word; do the work of an evangelist.* Do it under the anointing of the Holy Spirit. Beware of seeking to induce guilt by some mere psychological technique. Neither clever oratory, nor logical persuasion, nor angry denunciation of sin can move sinners to repentance. It is the power of God, working through the Holy Spirit, who will bring people to the Cross. We should be His willing tools to fulfill the evangelistic aspect of our calling.

The story is told of a world-famous violinist who earned a fortune with his concerts and compositions, but he generously gave most of it away. So, when he discovered an exquisite violin on one of his trips, he wasn't able to buy it. Later, having raised enough money to meet the asking price, he returned to the seller, hoping to purchase the beautiful instrument. But to his great dismay, it had been sold to a collector. The violinist made his way to the new owner's home and offered to buy the violin. The collector said it had become his prized possession and he would not sell it. Keenly disappointed, the violinist was about to leave when he had an idea. "Could I play the instrument once more before it is consigned to silence?" he asked. Permission was granted, and the great virtuoso filled the room with such heart-moving music that the collector's emotions were deeply stirred. "I have no right to keep that to myself," he exclaimed. "It's yours. Take it into the world, and let people hear it."

God has committed to us the ministry of reconciliation. We do not have the option of keeping quiet or neglecting to announce the good news. Do the work of an evangelist! Take the message to the world, and let people hear it.

## The Victory of Evangelistic Preaching

The calling to every preacher to be an evangelistic preacher is captured in Christ's words of the Great Commission. By reading it in the final chapters of each of the four Gospels and in the first chapter of Acts, we can get a full view of all its dimensions.

### He Says, "Go in My Power."

On the basis of who Jesus is and what He has done, He possesses power, which He promises those who obey His Commission. In the powerful imagery of 2 Corinthians 2:12-17, the declaration of the gospel is portrayed against the backdrop of a victorious Roman military parade. The heroes of the battle march into the city in their martial splendor. Behind the soldiers follow the captives. The city celebrates with shouts and the waving of burning incense. It is an aroma of victory for the army, but an aroma of death for the ones who have been enslaved. Such is the evangelistic sermon. For those who gladly accept the good tidings, it is an aroma of life; to those who close their ears and hearts, it is an aroma of death.

"Who is sufficient for these things?" asks Paul (v. 16). It's a question that might occur to today's evangelistic preacher. How can I do this? Jesus says we can do it, because we do it in His power. "All authority has been given to Me in heaven and on earth" (Matt. 28:18). We preach and issue an invitation in His name, because He told us to do it.

In 2 Corinthians 5:20, Paul asserts his authority by considering himself an ambassador for King Jesus. An *ambassador* is one who represents his ruler at the court of another. He speaks in the king's name. He makes agreements based on the authority of his ruler, which has been conferred upon him. His decisions are as binding as if the king himself had made them. His assurances are as firm as if they had come from the lips of his ruler. He has all authority.

The evangelistic preacher, too, speaks with the conviction and authority of the One whom he represents. He heralds the message of the King, and he is worthy of the dignity and deference owed to the Lord Jesus. All power—no limits, no restrictions. It is an aroma of life or an aroma of death. We are sufficient to bring the message and expect a positive response to it, because we speak for the King.

### He Says, "Go in My Program."

The purpose for which the preacher is sent is singular and specific: it is to make disciples. The construction of the Great Commission in Matthew 28:19-20 is instructive. Four verbs appear in the passage, but in Greek three of them are participles. Although "Go," as translated into English, gives the appearance of being an imperative, it is not an imperative in the Greek. Its more precise English interpretation would be "Going," or "As you are going." *Baptizing* and *teaching* join their fellow-helping verb—*going, baptizing, teaching.* There is only one imperative: *matheteusate*—"make disciples"! We follow His command most meticulously when our principal task is making disciples; that is, giving an evangelistic invitation wherever we go, and following it up with baptizing and teaching. That kind of ministry produces disciples.

What Christ commissions His church to do is "make disciples." In order to do so, there must be some "going." We have to go to where sinners are, either next door or across the world. There must be "baptizing," which signals the incorporation of the new believer into the body of Christ, the family of the church. There must be "teaching," which instructs the Christian about the truth to believe and the way to live. But the heart of the matter is "make disciples." Turn people from darkness to light.

## Spirit-Filled Preaching Is Evangelistic

Where they have previously lived for their own purposes (or for no purpose at all), they now live for His purposes.

The great work of the church is to win men and women to become His followers. The pulpit still offers the preacher his supreme evangelistic opportunity. Henry Crocker captured the calling in a poem:

> Give us a watchword for this hour,
> A thrilling word, a word of power,
> A battle-cry, a flaming breath
> That calls to conquest or to death.
> A word to rouse the Church from rest,
> To hear her Master's high request.
> A call is given, ye hosts arise,
> Our watchword is *evangelize.*

Jesus says He will honor our efforts as we follow His program.

### He Says, "Go in My Presence."

A delightful assurance that Jesus adds at the end of the Great Commission is the promise of His presence with His obedient people until the end of the age.

*Living in His presence assures fruitfulness.* Jesus makes clear that our utter dependence on abiding with Him will help us bring forth fruit:

> "Abide in Me, and I in you. As the branch cannot bear fruit of itself, unless it abides in the vine, neither can you, unless you abide in Me. I am the vine, you are the branches. He who abides in Me, and I in him, bears much fruit; for without Me you can do nothing" (John 15:4-5).

*Living in His presence brings assurance.* "I'm going to be gone away for a while," Jesus tells His followers, "but I'm going to prepare a place where you can live with Me, and I'll come back and get you" (see John 14:1-4). In the meantime, He made it clear that they should not be troubled or afraid. His presence would be with them in the person of the Comforter, the Holy

Spirit: "Peace I leave with you, My peace I give to you; not as the world gives do I give to you. Let not your heart be troubled, neither let it be afraid" (v. 27). When we are living in His presence, doing His will, we possess assurance and peace.

*Living in His presence guarantees strength.* When we live in His presence, it puts us in the presence of like-minded brothers and sisters, who also live in His presence, and that can be a tremendous source of encouragement. A threefold cord is not easily broken.

Gardner Taylor, the wonderful preacher and professor of preaching, sums up preaching in a message about the valley of dry bones in Ezekiel 37, recounted in his book *How Shall They Preach?* Of course, the primary application of the text is to the return of the Jews to their land. Perhaps, though, it can also be relevant to the business of preaching evangelistically. What do you think?

> Wherever one's preaching lot is cast, there will be men and women long in captivity. . . . In darkened cells of the spirit, half dead, they sit. And, then . . . they see the running feet of the courier and know by his garments that he is the King's messenger. They know also that he bears welcome and long longed-for word of the mighty battle and a great victory, and that because of that victory soon their cell doors will swing wide and they will stand free in the sunlight once again.[3]

Isaiah declared, "How beautiful upon the mountains are the feet of him who brings good news, who proclaims peace, who bring glad tidings of good things" (52:7).

Preach the Word! Do the work of an evangelist! Deliver the good tidings. God commands it. People need it. Obedience demands it. Heaven rewards it. "Now then, we are ambassadors for Christ, as though God were pleading through us: we implore you on Christ's behalf, be reconciled to God" (2 Cor. 5:20).

# 5

# Spirit-Filled Preaching Will Have Signs Following

Timothy M. Hill

*"And these signs will follow those who believe: In My name they will cast out demons; they will speak with new tongues; they will take up serpents; and if they drink anything deadly, it will by no means hurt them; they will lay hands on the sick, and they will recover"* (Mark 16:17-18).

That Spirit-filled preaching will have signs following is an unquestionable truth, supported throughout the Word of God. One needs only to look at the miracles of the Old Testament to know that God has always worked in miraculous ways when His Word is honored and proclaimed. The fiery exhortations of the Old Testament prophets frequently were accompanied by powerful miracles—the dead were raised to life again, lepers were cleansed, a cruse flowed with a perpetual oil supply, a river's raging waters stopped flowing so God's people could cross, the Red Sea parted so the Israelites could escape Pharaoh's pursuing army. These are only a few of the many miracles recorded by the Old Testament writers.

### Miracles in the New Testament

The earthly ministry of Jesus was a miracle ministry. He turned water into wine, restored withered limbs, opened blind eyes, stopped a funeral procession, emptied tombs, made the

*Scriptures are from the *New King James Version* unless otherwise indicated.

lame walk, and cast out demons. "And there are also many other things that Jesus did, which if they were written one by one, I suppose that even the world itself could not contain the books that would be written" (John 21:25).

Jesus commissioned His disciples to engage in miracle ministry: "He called the twelve to Himself, and began to send them out two by two, and gave them power over unclean spirits. . . . So they went out and preached that people should repent. And they cast out many demons, and anointed with oil many who were sick, and healed them" (Mark 6:7, 12-13). Two of the signs following believers recorded in chapter 16 were prominent in the ministry of Jesus' disciples—casting out demons and healing the sick.

Jesus empowered His church to proclaim the gospel when He said, "You shall receive power when the Holy Spirit has come upon you; and you shall be witnesses to Me in Jerusalem, and in all Judea and Samaria, and to the end of the earth" (Acts 1:8). Filled with the Holy Spirit, the early church's ministers preached the message of Christ with great power, and with signs following.

Miracles, notable healings, and the free operation of the gifts of the Spirit accompanied the preaching of the apostles. These same signs will accompany Spirit-filled preaching today. Jesus gave His followers a command to "go into all the world and preach the gospel," and He promised "these signs will follow those who believe: In My name they will cast out demons; they will speak with new tongues; they will take up serpents; and if they drink anything deadly, it will by no means hurt them; they will lay hands on the sick, and they will recover" (Mark 16:15, 17-18).

According to Jesus, Spirit-filled preachers are to preach the gospel—the good news of salvation through faith in Christ. Further, they are to preach everywhere—all the world—and they are to baptize their converts. Signs can be expected to follow their preaching, confirming the preached word. After receiving this charge from the Lord, the apostles "went out and preached everywhere, the Lord working with them and confirming the word through the accompanying signs" (v. 20). Why do we not have more signs and wonders accompanying preaching today? Could it be that the Lord is not "working with us" because the unadulterated Word of God is no longer being preached from many pulpits?

The apostle Paul declared, "For I will not dare to speak of any of those things which Christ has not accomplished through me, in word and deed, to make the Gentiles obedient—in mighty signs and wonders, by the power of the Spirit of God, so that from Jerusalem and round about to Illyricum I have fully preached the gospel of Christ" (Rom. 15:18-19). Paul emphasized that "in mighty signs and wonders, by the power of the Spirit of God . . . [he had] fully preached the gospel of Christ" (v. 19).

Paul also told the Corinthian church, "My speech and my preaching were not with persuasive words of human wisdom, but in demonstration of the Spirit and of power, that your faith should not be in the wisdom of men but in the power of God" (1 Cor. 2:4-5).

## Spirit-Filled Preaching Is Powerful and Effective

Spirit-filled preaching, then, is powerful and effective, and is accompanied and confirmed by mighty signs and wonders, which are wrought by the power of the Spirit of God. The writer of Hebrews declared, "God also bearing witness both with signs and wonders, with various miracles, and gifts of the Holy Spirit" (2:4).

The following is taken from my book *Beyond the Mist*:

> There is still a place for the fivefold ministry to function in the church. Too often, the church is dysfunctional, because we are not allowing these ministries to play their important

role of bringing maturity to the body of Christ. We need apostolic covering today that raises up sons and daughters in church-planting ministries around the world.

And, where is the voice of the prophet? I'm not talking about the self-proclaimed, but those whose prophetic voice is made valid by the fruit of what they have spoken coming to pass. This nation needs to hear a "thus saith the Lord."

The evangelists must come out of hiding, too. Where are the John the Baptists of this generation? Where are those who are not afraid to point the church back to repentance? Evangelists have a calling that is unique and can't be carried by just anyone. They are a gift to the body that should be celebrated and utilized. The pastors and teachers have primarily been shouldering the load, because the church hasn't known how to incorporate the other three gifts and offices. While the pastor and teacher have done well to advance ministry in the church, still the church has been greatly hindered by the lack of these gifts operating in the body. But from this story of the daughter of Jairus, we see what happens when all the gifts are functioning properly—resurrection, restoration, and healing come to the body.

The Bible said that after Jesus spoke to the girl, "her spirit returned" (Luke 8:55). What a miracle! She had a body, but she did not have a spirit. She had the form, but she did not have power. So it is across America today. There are many bodies called churches, but too little spirit. The Spirit must come back to the church, for "in Him we live and move and have our being" (Acts 17:28).

The girl was brought to life, but she needed nourishment. Jesus instructed her parents, the pastor, and the teacher, "to give her meat" (Luke 8:55 KJV). What a challenge! He was about to do an accelerated work that demanded more than the typical meal of soup and bread. You would think that after the traumatic experience of being sick and dying, Jesus would have instructed her parents to move ever so slowly with her. Not at all. There was a powerful work to be done in her generation.

God is calling on church leaders and shepherds to give this generation the "meat" of His Word. This generation needs more than our watered-down nursery rhymes, our meaningless clichés, and our half-baked sermons. There is an accelerated work for this new generation, and we dare not give them anything less than the truth of God's Word. The new generation is an anointed generation that will lay hands on the sick and cast out devils. They will prophesy and speak to nations. They will not put up with business as usual or church as usual. The new generation will make a difference and ultimately usher in the King of kings.

Imagine that after Jesus raised up this child, He said to her, "Wait here. I have someone that I want you to meet." And suppose He went and found the woman He had healed from the issue of blood (see Luke 8:43-44) and brought the two together, because the young twelve-year-old girl had an "experience," but the older woman had a "testimony." The world needed to see both. Once healed, the older woman had a story that could help bring maturity to the younger.

In the process that God uses to bring about a revived church, it is important that the older generation pass on a testimony of faithfulness to be combined with the passionate resurrection experience of the new. What a powerful combination when the two are brought together. How powerful? The potential is revealed in the opening verses of Luke 9. Following the healing of a woman who was sick for twelve years and the resurrection of a twelve-year-old girl, Jesus then gave new instructions to His twelve disciples. The number *12* speaks of order, government, and alignment. It speaks of the church operating in proper order. According to verses 1 and 2, once everything was in order, He then gave them authority and power over the devil, as well as the ability to deliver from all manner of diseases. They were sent to preach the Kingdom and heal the sick.

A healthy church will impact the world and bring deliverance through the name of Jesus to everyone who believes.[1]

## The Revival at Samaria

"Then Philip went down to the city of Samaria and preached Christ to them. And the multitudes with one accord heeded the things spoken by Philip, hearing and seeing the miracles which he did. For unclean spirits, crying with a loud voice, came out of many who were possessed; and many who were paralyzed and lame were healed. And there was great joy in that city" (Acts 8:5-8).

These verses record one of the notable early instances of Spirit-filled preaching accompanied by signs following. A persecution had arisen against the Christians in Jerusalem, which resulted in a number of them leaving the city and going to other areas. One such individual was Philip, who chose to go to Samaria, a city considered off-limits by most of the Jews, since the Samaritans were a mixed-blood group who disputed the proper place of worship with the Jews. Jews who were traveling in the area would go the long way around in order to avoid going through Samaria.

But Philip went to Samaria, and there he preached Jesus Christ. The people of the city heard and heeded Philip's preaching, which evidently was delivered with Spirit-filled power. Philip's preaching was accompanied by miracles, which were witnessed by the people. "For unclean spirits, crying with a loud voice, came out of many who were possessed; and many who were paralyzed and lame were healed" (v. 7). The signs that followed Philip's preaching were of such power and effect that "there was great joy in that city" (v. 8).

Prominent among the signs following Spirit-filled preaching in apostolic times were tongues, casting out demons, and healing—although the miraculous signs certainly were not limited only to these. In his *Ecclesiastical History*, Eusebius Pamphilus, bishop of Cesarea, recorded: "For Thomas, under a divine impulse, sent Thaddeus as herald and evangelist, to proclaim the doctrine of Christ, as we have shown from the public documents found there. When he came to these places, he both healed Agbarus by the word of Christ, and astonished all there with the extraordinary miracles he performed."[2]

## Christ Is the Focus of Spirit-Filled Preaching

Frank Bartleman, an eyewitness and reporter in the midst of the phenomenal move of God's power known as the Azusa Street Revival, stated in 1906: "We may not hold a doctrine, or seek an experience, except in Christ. Many are willing to seek power in order to perform miracles, draw attention and adoration of the people to themselves, thus robbing Christ of His glory and making a fair showing in the flesh. . . . We must stick to our text—Jesus Christ."[3]

Take note of some more of Bartleman's astounding warnings:

> Any work that exalts the Holy Ghost or "gifts" above Jesus will finally end up in fanaticism. Whatever causes us to exalt and love Jesus is well and safe. The reverse will ruin all. The Holy Ghost is a great light, but always focused on Jesus and always for His revealing. Where the Holy Ghost is actually in control, Jesus is proclaimed the Head—the Holy Ghost His Executive. . . . We must not put power, gifts, the Holy Ghost or, in fact anything, ahead of Jesus. Any mission that exalts even the Holy Ghost above the Lord Jesus Christ is bound for the rocks of error and fanaticism. . . . The Holy Ghost will never draw our attention from Christ to Himself, but rather reveal Christ in a fuller way. Jesus must be the center of everything.[4]

It is always my hope that in every service where I minister, spiritual gifts will be in operation. The gifts of faith and healing, along with speaking with tongues and the interpretation of these tongues, serve as a strength and reinforcement to my faith. But none of these can operate at the expense of Christ's lordship. Those gifts do not operate so that I can become popular and sell books. Concerning the gifts, Paul wrote, "But one and the same Spirit works all these things, distributing to each one individually as He wills" (1 Cor. 12:11). The gifts operate in the Church to bring glory to the name of Jesus and to edify His body. When we look back on our worship experiences, we must be able to testify that Jesus was affirmed at His rightful place of lordship in His church.

Who doesn't want to have a powerful ministry and be effective? I for one want the power of God to emanate from my life onto others when I minister. However, nothing can happen in that regard until first I have embraced purity and holy living before the Lord. It's an old sermon that most experienced preachers have already preached long ago, but it still rings with truth and relevance today: that is, too many want to go straight to the Upper Room in Jerusalem without first stopping at Calvary. The Old Testament priest could not even go into the Holy Place without first stopping at the brazen altar. How shall we expect any less responsibility in our preparation to stand before a holy God? Many preachers are promoting power ministries, but few will preach about the power of holiness. Yet, the Bible plainly declares, "Pursue peace with all people, and holiness, without which no one will see the Lord" (Heb. 12:14). Popularity wanes when you preach about sin rather than success. Regardless, holiness is still God's standard of living for His people.

## There Is No Shortcut to Authentic Revival

In a day when the Father is so anxious to touch people's hearts, why would anyone attempt to fabricate, manipulate, and "scheme up" a revival? While disappointing, it's not surprising, because even shortly after Pentecost, men attempted to find shortcuts to revival.

Two incidents recorded in the Book of Acts have remarkable similarities to the approach some take today. One involved a man's mistaken notion that power with God is on the open market and can be bought at a bargain price. The other involved an immature conglomerate of would-be exorcists. They thought a distant connection with God and the skill of name-dropping could get them anywhere, while making demons tremble along the way. I am referring to an individual known as Simon the sorcerer and also seven young men identified as sons of the chief priest, Sceva.

Acts 8:9-24 tells of Simon's story. Here is his introduction:

> There was a certain man called Simon, who previously practiced sorcery in the city and astonished the people of Samaria, claiming that he was someone great, to whom they all gave heed, from the least to the greatest, saying, "This man is the

great power of God." And they heeded him because he had astonished them with his sorceries for a long time (vv. 9-11).

These verses reveal the following diagnosis of a spiritually unfit man:
- Simon was a *sensationalist*, who played on the emotions of people.
- He was an *egotist*, making bold claims about his own importance and ability.
- He was a *deceptionist*, allowing people to credit him as God's agent of great miracle-working power.
- Finally, he was an *opportunist*, who thought that with enough money, a person could buy his way to evangelical and miracle "stardom."

When Simon saw that through the laying on of the apostles' hands the Holy Spirit was given, he offered them money, saying, "Give me this power also, that anyone on whom I lay hands may receive the Holy Spirit." But Peter said to him, "Your money perish with you, because you thought that the gift of God could be purchased with money! You have neither part nor portion in this matter, for your heart is not right in the sight of God. Repent therefore of this your wickedness, and pray God if perhaps the thought of your heart may be forgiven you. For I see that you are poisoned by bitterness and bound by iniquity" (vv. 18-23).

## Showmanship Cannot Replace Authenticity

The faithful and consecrated ministries in the world today far outnumber those of a questionable and suspicious nature. There are men and women who have completely given themselves to serving God by helping His people, and the only reward they seek is to please the Lord by displaying the proof of a faithful life. On the other hand, there have been far too many "plastic" preachers who have sold enough evangelical "snake oil" to last a lifetime. I've received enough unsolicited Holy Land "miracle water" to float a boat and enough "money-green" handkerchiefs to quilt a blanket. These kinds of ministries fail the test of authenticity, and grieve the Holy Spirit as they take advantage of good people. Somewhere along the road of their ministries, anointing and power were replaced with showmanship and gimmicks.

Scripture records that when called into accountability, Simon asked to be forgiven. Though Luke chose not to record the resulting conclusion, we can hope that Simon did repent and become credible in his walk with God and before all people. I pray that men and women who started out with great humility and then became victimized by Satan's "pride trap" will soon return to a broken and contrite spirit that God can use once again.

Now consider the seven sons of Sceva. They too failed the authenticity test. Acts 19:11-16 conveys the story:

> Now God worked unusual miracles by the hands of Paul, so that even handkerchiefs or aprons were brought from his body to the sick, and the diseases left them and the evil spirits went out of them. Then some of the itinerant Jewish exorcists took it upon themselves to call the name of the Lord Jesus over those who had evil spirits, saying, "We exorcise you by the Jesus whom Paul preaches." Also there were seven sons of Sceva, a Jewish chief priest, who did so. And the evil spirit answered and said, "Jesus I know, and Paul I know; but who are you?" Then the man in whom the evil spirit was leaped on them, overpowered them, and prevailed against them, so that they fled out of that house naked and wounded.

They wielded a name, but they had no relationship. Surely, Satan must have laughed as they boldly proclaimed to the demon-possessed, "By the Jesus whom Paul preaches, we command you to come out!" Who knows—God himself may have even chuckled at that one! The Bible does say that under certain circumstances He will laugh in the day of calamity. I would say this encounter certainly qualified as one of those days for these young men. Who knows if it was arrogance, ignorance, presumption, or just blatant stupidity.

Whatever it was, it didn't work, and they should have known better. After all, they had a religious, though apparently not very spiritual, upbringing. They learned the hard way that a person can throw a name around all day long, but if there is no relationship to back it up, all they will get out of it is embarrassment. People may come and see your show, buy your "devil-busting kit," and ask for you to sign their Bibles; but when the real devil shows up, you had better have more than a formula and an emotional outburst. Somewhere, there had better be a Christ-in-you relationship that will make the powers of darkness tremble and flee when you are seen coming through the door.

On one occasion, the disciples came to Jesus exuberant because they had cast out demons in His name. The Master quickly focused them on the greater issue by saying the higher cause for rejoicing rested in the fact that their names were written in the Lamb's Book of Life (see Luke 10:17-20; Rev. 21:27).

## Build Your Life on a Relationship With Jesus

If you are a young pastor or evangelist, or even a young father or mother starting your family, please read the next few words carefully: Build your life, ministry, and family on a relationship with Jesus. It is not enough to know His name, as highly exalted as it is; you must know *Him*. The only way to have longevity in ministry is to know *Him*. I will take knowing *Him* over titles, positions, and applause. How is your relationship with *Him*?

Sceva's seven sons pursued manifestations that they hoped would validate their own importance. It is obvious by Scripture that these young men had a desire to be seen as significant players in the Kingdom, but unfortunately they placed their personal worth in the kind of outward manifestations that followed their ministry. It seems they had formed their own association for exorcists so they could run together and even "gang up" on the devil. It is really sad, but the truth is, some people won't go to a revival service unless they know there will be some display of spiritual gifts before the night is over.

Please understand, I believe in the operational gifts of the Spirit. I've seen some indescribable things happen around the world as people came into the presence of God. But long ago, I realized my value as a minister can only be determined by my level of discipleship with Christ. How God uses me as an evangelist, pastor, or leader will flow out of my walk with Jesus.

Jesus said there will always be those who will follow after signs. Others will come only for the "loaves and fishes." The church has always had spiritual "fire truck and ambulance chasers." Granted, excitement does draw a crowd. Once, I pastored a church where just a few years before I arrived, they had printed bumper stickers that read, "The Exciting Church in Town." I never did like that sticker and refused to put one on my car. I don't like bumper stickers anyway, but I would have preferred one that said, "A Faithful Church in Town."

## Miracles Do Not Validate Your Importance

Your importance is not validated by miracles. Your value to the body of Christ is not determined by your unusual feats of spiritual performance. Your value is found in your love and loyalty to Jesus Christ, your faithfulness to preach His Word, and your burden to care for His children. If you have these traits, you'll never have to worry about flunking the authenticity test.

Consider Elijah, who passed his test with flying colors. He took the exam on top of Mount Carmel, with 850 false prophets breathing down his neck. This dramatic story is told in 1 Kings 18. From this story about one man's authenticity test, we learn the following principles:

1. *Never determine your difficulty by the size of the opposition.* Elijah was outnumbered by his enemies, but he knew with God on his side, he was really in the majority. Our unseen God is always mightier than every visible foe. Don't forget that if God is for you, no one can successfully stand against you.
2. *Where there is no sacrifice, there can be no fire.* Elijah called for the repairing of the altar. Once the altar had

been rebuilt, he called for a trench to be dug around it, into which twelve barrels of water were poured. Water was precious in a land where no rain had fallen for three years. On top of the altar, Elijah placed the blood-soaked offering and stood back and waited on God to reveal His awesome glory. Elijah passed the consecration test.

3. *Someone who prays long in private can pray briefly in public and still get the job done.* Have you ever counted the words contained in Elijah's prayer that day? Sixty words—that's it. They were strong and anointed words, but honestly, I can point you to more eloquent words and prayers throughout the Bible. It wasn't so much *what* was said as much as *who* said it. This man had a powerful communion with God. When he spoke, heaven stood at attention and gave heed to Elijah's voice of intercession. The results are seen in these words: "Then the fire of the Lord fell" (v. 38). He passed the communion test.

Earlier, I stated that any religion can be thought to be a good religion until it is called upon to produce something. Elijah's encounter with the prophets of Baal proves this to be true. They also had built altars. They had prayed all day, cut themselves, jumped up and down, and screamed aloud the entire time. But they failed the test, and couldn't produce a thing. They were not authentic. They were a devil-devised flesh parade that had brought a nation to its darkest days. Their influence wilted when brought against a true move of God's power.

## We Must Prove Our Authenticity

The church is on trial today. We stand at the judgment bar of a generation that will not be sympathetic to old excuses. They will not endure our arguments, and they will not wait while we try to reinvent ourselves. If we can't prove our authenticity, then this generation will simply move on, wagging their heads in mournful pity of a church lost in a fog, content in a mist.

We must ask ourselves: Can our ministries pass the test of authenticity? Can our praying produce the fire of God that consumes our sacrificed pride? Do our values reflect the Christ-life to the world?

The church must accept the fact that ecstasy does not equate to revival. We must also recognize that real revival will change the spiritual climate of the church as well as the nation. A. W. Tozer said, "I contend that whatever does not raise the moral standard of the church or community has not been a revival from God."[5] Vance Havner described revival as "falling in love with Jesus all over again."[6] Anything less will fail the test of authenticity.

"Authentic imitations" will produce "authentic limitations," and until the church takes hold of that fact, we will continue to bump our heads against the lid of frustrated and unrealized dreams. Like day and night, there is a difference between a church in revival and one that only spins around in an exhausting display of carnal effort and prideful assumption. The world knows the difference, and Jesus does as well. Seven times, and to seven different congregations, Jesus said, "I know your works" (Rev. 2; 3).

The Lord is looking for authenticity, and only those who produce it will have significance in this generation. Legitimacy and credibility in spiritual matters sets the church apart from the rest of the world.

Spirit-filled preaching does indeed have signs following that confirm the preached Word. But our preaching must always be centered on Christ. Then, and only then, will the signs following our ministries have authenticity and point people to Jesus.

# 6

# Spirit-Filled Preaching Makes Disciples

### Alton Garrison

*"Therefore go and make disciples of all the nations, baptizing them in the name of the Father and of the Son and of the Holy Spirit"* (Matt. 28:19).

In describing the state of the Great Commission today, Dr. John Perkins famously said, "We have over-evangelized the world too lightly."[1] When asked what the phrase meant, he said evangelism actually becomes counterproductive to God's purpose for the Church when it is not partnered with discipleship. Evangelism and discipleship should be inseparable aims of the Church.

Don't misunderstand me; salvation is imperative. Scripture is clear that there is a basic starting point to the Christian faith: admitting we need Jesus and then accepting Him as Savior. God is "not willing that any should perish, but that all should come to repentance" (2 Peter 3:9 KJV). However, the starting point should not become a substitute for the divinely ordained process to follow—Christian discipleship.

Intentionally or not, we have promoted the idea that being a Christ-follower is primarily about the choice to convert. We do not portray it as an all-out, into-the-Kingdom enlistment that dramatically influences every corner of life. Our myopic focus on the starting point comes at a cost to the greater portion of the Christian experience that should otherwise follow. "In a get-saved culture, too many of the conversions become either 'aborted' believers or casual Christians."[2] Barna's research shows that

---

*Scriptures are from the *New International Version* unless otherwise indicated.

most of the respondents in one study who made a decision for Christ were no longer connected to a Christian church within a short period of time following their initial decision, usually eight to twelve weeks.[3]

To change the perception that we, as ministers of the gospel, are focused only on converts, we must embrace a more holistic idea of what it means to be a Christ-follower. This requires that we focus our attention on spiritual formation, but even more fundamental than our calling to promote and nourish this process must be our own commitment to be spiritually formed. Spirit-filled preaching that makes disciples is contingent upon the Holy Spirit's transformation of preachers into disciples themselves. These are powerfully married principles.

Paul the apostle could write to the Corinthians, "Follow my example, as I follow the example of Christ" (1 Cor. 11:1). Paul did not issue that invitation from a position of spiritual perfection. He freely admitted to the Philippian believers that he continued to strive for a deeper relationship with Christ and had not yet attained all that he knew that relationship to be (Phil. 3:10-14). The more the Holy Spirit transformed Paul, the more equipped he became to urge new converts to pursue lives of dedicated discipleship.

I saw this truth powerfully demonstrated in the life and ministry of my father. His legacy continues to shape my own life and ministry. As I share his story, I want to connect the testimony to four principles of Pentecostal preaching—principles that elicit a response of growing discipleship when followers of Christ are receptive to the Holy Spirit's prodding toward maturity.

## The Work of the Spirit Is Discipleship's Foundation

Before my father was known across our community as Pastor C. H. Garrison, he was far better known as an alcoholic. An oilfield worker, he had dropped out of school in the tenth grade and endured a very dysfunctional life of hard work—when he could keep a job—and equally hard drinking.

C. H. and Alese Garrison were married when he was thirty and she was eighteen. They did not have children for seven years, during which his drinking rarely abated. Had I been born and raised in that environment, I almost certainly would not have found God's path for my life. But when I was about to be born, under the influence of the Holy Spirit to which my dad was completely oblivious, he began to get serious about quitting drinking.

While Dad tried unsuccessfully to give up alcohol, he was only marginally successful at holding down a job. When he was able to find work, he would hide his paycheck in an attempt to keep from spending it all on drink. Inevitably, he would find the check and spend it all in a night. He averaged a fifth of whiskey a day.

About six months before I was born, my parents had been to a Fourth of July celebration. Dad had been drinking. He and Mom were headed home in southeast Texas where they lived. As Dad drove, he suddenly felt as if he were having a heart attack. His fear was if he died, he would wreck the car and kill Mom and the baby they were expecting. Without explaining to Mom why, he slowed the car down and began to plead with God.

"I don't know how to pray," he said under his breath, "but my mother used to pray. If You heard her prayer, maybe You'll hear mine. Spare my life to see my child; save me. And if I ever take another drop of liquor for as long as I live, I want You to poison me and let me drop dead."

At that moment, Jesus Christ looked beyond all of my father's past failures, and He healed, saved, and completely delivered him in that moment.

So, when I quote John Perkins' analysis that we have "over-evangelized the world too lightly," I am in no way devaluing the initial miracle of salvation. As Jesus so clearly taught in His discourse with Nicodemus, the miracle of the new birth is the crux on which everything rests when it comes to our eternal destiny (John 3:1-21). Just as clearly, Jesus identifies this miracle as a work of the Holy Spirit (vv. 5-8).

Dad was baptized in the Holy Spirit just weeks later. Here again, the Spirit's work is fundamental to every growth process in the Christian life. Dad's life changed, and he gave up smoking and other destructive habits. His two sisters had also been saved and were attending a little independent Pentecostal church in Sour Lake, near Beaumont and just a short drive from the Gulf Coast.

The church was still getting on its feet when the pastor left, so Dad and his two sisters went to nearby Beaumont to meet with Harry H. Hodge, pastor of Sabine Tabernacle and founder of United Gospel Tabernacles. As they appealed to Brother Hodge to send another pastor to Sour Lake, he looked at Dad and said, "There's your pastor." Dad had only come as the driver. He looked around in surprise. He had only recently come to Christ and had been a hopeless drunk only months before. Brother Hodge told Dad, "Go home and pray about it; and when God speaks to you what He spoke to me, you come back."

In a couple of weeks, Dad returned to Beaumont and was appointed pastor of the Sour Lake church. He had never finished high school . . . never been to Bible college . . . never preached a sermon. And he was the pastor of a church.

Dad stayed in that church twenty-two years. Just a few years ago, my wife, Johanna, and I went back to preach an anniversary there. It is still not a large church—just a little white building that holds about ninety people—but the lives that have been impacted and the testimonies coming from that congregation speak of an astounding and continuing work of the Spirit.

Here's my point. While my dad's situation was certainly exceptional—his having no education to speak of—we know that the Holy Spirit can compensate for our inadequacies.

# Discipleship Demands Evidence of the Spirit's Work

Particularly in the American church experience, there is a wide disconnect between talk of discipleship and actual discipleship. In his book *unChristian*, David Kinnaman writes:

> In virtually every study we conduct, representing thousands of interviews every year, born-again Christians fail to display much attitudinal or behavioral evidence of transformed lives. For instance, based on a study released in 2007, we found that most of the lifestyle activities of born-again Christians were statistically equivalent to those of non-born-agains. When asked to identify their activities over the last thirty days, born-again believers were just as likely to bet or gamble, to visit a pornographic website, to take something that did not belong to them, to consult a medium or psychic, to physically fight or abuse someone, to have consumed enough alcohol to be considered legally drunk, to have used an illegal, nonprescription drug, to have said something to someone that was not true, to have gotten back at someone for something he or she did, and to have said mean things behind another person's back.[4]

The Gospels reveal that Jesus was very specific in His expectations of disciples. When He commanded the apostles to "make disciples," He expected the following responsibilities.[5]

## Commitment

"Anyone who does not carry his cross and follow me cannot be my disciple" (Luke 14:27).

We can learn in groups, serve in teams, and worship as a family; but we can only be disciples individually. Without commitment, discipleship cannot happen; and the level of that commitment cannot be a percentage. The call for a personal cross is a call for absolute abandon to the will of God in our lives, a call to obey Him regardless of the cost.

## Competence

"If you remain in me and my words remain in you, ask whatever you wish, and it will be given you. This is to my Father's glory, that you bear much fruit, showing yourselves to be my disciples" (John 15:7-8). How often that verse has been manipulated to appear as some lunch ticket to endless prosperity! But look at the intended result of the fruitful prayer—bearing much fruit.

Jesus invites all who put their trust in Him to move through life in deep fellowship with Him as they carry out His mission in the world. To that end, when they ask anything of the Father, He grants it—wisdom, skill, and, yes, material resources to bring about Kingdom goals. The truly competent believer, the one who is observing fruitful increase daily, is the disciple who remains in intimate fellowship with the Savior and in deep interaction with His Word.

## Character

"A new command I give you: Love one another. As I have loved you, so you must love one another. By this all men will know that you are my disciples, if you love one another" (John 13:34-35).

Preachers are famous for hanging out a laundry list of dos and don'ts for the Christian life. While Scripture does go into detail on the characteristics of true followers of Christ, every one of those qualities is contingent on one point of character Jesus himself emphasized—love.

You can spend all day evaluating your own discipleship progress—or the progress of your congregation—with spiritual laundry lists. When you zero in on love and determine whether or not it is the motivation for everything taking place in your life and in your congregation, you have found the single greatest key to the character of the true disciple.

## Conviction

"You shall know the truth, and the truth shall make you free" (John 8:32 NKJV). Too often, Christians are knowledge-rich and application-poor. Freedom comes through the application of knowledge, through putting it into practice.

We pride ourselves in having "right" doctrine; but without conviction—the kind that leads to commitment, competence, and character development—our lifestyles differ little from the cultural norm and do not even hint at Christ within us.

## Pentecostal Preaching Creates Discipleship Opportunities

As the evidence of discipleship becomes clear in our own lives, we can then stand before a group of disciples who are at various destinations on their own faith journeys and encourage them to continue along a spiritually fruitful path. Let me break down a discipleship-motivating sermon into five components.

### 1. Connection Time

Jesus personally connected with His disciples. That relational dynamic lies at the root of how the Master invested Himself in the Twelve. Your relationships with the believers under your spiritual care are a vital component to their growth as disciples. You must, then, preach relationally.

Some pastors who are more relational may spend a few more minutes setting up the connection time before delivering the first key point of the sermon. Connection time is important as well when a message is a part of a series. You can look back to previous messages and forward to future messages.

"Communicators" will differ from "speakers" in this area. Communicators will use the audience response to measure the connection time. Speakers will simply move forward without gauging how they have connected with their audiences.

Connection time establishes how the speaker will create an environment for the Holy Spirit to work through the preaching of the Word. Connection time is very important and should be the transitional catalyst for the preaching.

## 2. Defining the Objective

As you begin to unpack the message, remember to define your objective. If the subject is *evangelism*, there might be fifteen different ideas of what you mean when you say "evangelism" to a congregation of one hundred people. Once people decide they know what you are going to talk about, they will lock into their idea of your topic and will have trouble adjusting if you are talking about a different concept. Be clear at the beginning as to where you intend to go with your message, and they can stay on course with you throughout.

If you spend a few quality minutes explaining your objective, you can keep everyone on the same page. Defining the objective also gives you the ability to fit the objective into your series framework so they see how this message will connect to those given previously.

Think back over the last three messages you preached. Did you provide the objective for each message, or did you assume everyone knew what you were talking about? Assumptions will kill the opportunity for clarity and may find you spending more time clarifying than if you had defined the objective in the beginning of the message.

## 3. Biblical Reference Points

*Biblical reference points* are the sustaining Scripture verses from the series or those chosen for use in the current message. These support the direction of the message, identify core life values from Scripture, and anchor any definitions in the message to a biblical position rather than one speaker's interpretation of Scripture.

Biblical reference points can be the difference between sharing an opinion and delivering the Word of God. These must not be individual verses pulled out of context. They should be clearly connected to larger biblical narratives, to doctrines established through the scriptural process, and to the vision and core values of the church.

Biblical reference points give you the opportunity to connect timeless Scripture with the world in which we live. You are helping your congregation discover—or rediscover—how the Word established through the millennia impacts and shapes and offers solutions to their immediate circumstances. You are unpacking the power behind the principles, you are revealing the presence of a divine plan, and you are pointing them to the possibilities for a victorious future.

**4. Application and Implementation**

After connecting personally with the congregation, defining the objective of a message, and giving scriptural support, many speakers measure the application and implementation by the altar-call response. However, if we were to look a little deeper, we would recognize the importance of applying the message in daily life after the church lights have been turned off for the weekend.

This is where true discipleship comes to life. Frankly, application and implementation are harder than they look. To clearly define for people how they should move forward in their personal life, business behavior, and church relationships can be overwhelming at times. That is why many pastors avoid the challenge and choose an evangelism altar call to give a wider opportunity for people to respond. We certainly must allow people to find Christ in our services, just as we also will pray for the sick and those facing other difficulties; but unless we connect our message with long-term life change, we are yet again "over-evangelizing the world too lightly."

We must connect believers to the future vision the Holy Spirit desires to speak into their lives, help them discover that every follower of Christ has some form of ministry calling, and offer nuts-and-bolts teaching through the fabric of our preaching week to week that calls them to repeatedly examine and fine-tune the direction of their daily lives. The application and implementation component should give a clear understanding of how the message can be lived out beyond the pews.

**5. Release**

The last component is to release each person to actively engage the message in their daily lives. It is the imparted realization that a sermon is not a chain tying the believer to a limited body of text and exposition shared on Sunday, but rather an invitation to explore infinite possibilities. The release should give each person the lasting impetus for discovery, discussion, and development for their individual lives, for their efforts as lay leaders, and for their participation in congregation and community life.

## Hope Sustains the Disciple

This life is a battering ram against our growth in faith and our progress as disciples. No wonder Jesus said to His disciples, "In this world you will have trouble. But take heart! I have overcome the world" (John 16:33). When Jesus said to "take heart," He was calling us to hope. He was addressing the deep emotional needs all of us have, emotions that often run in conflict with our foundation of faith. Let me illustrate that truth with a final chapter from my father's life.

After twenty-two years in Sour Lake, Mom and Dad moved to Lake Charles, Louisiana, where Dad pastored Calcasieu Tabernacle. After a decade there, Dad was stricken with Alzheimer's disease. It did not seem fair to me. He had served the Lord so faithfully, yet now it was an agonizing, seven-year struggle that left his mind and body destroyed.

I received a call to come to the care facility. My father was close to death. The doctor was leaving Dad's room as I arrived. He told me Dad was no longer with us for all practical purposes. All measurable brain function tied to cognition had ceased. Dad had not spoken for more than three months; it was physically impossible for him to speak. He was so close to death, but for some reason his body was hanging on.

The doctor fully expected Dad to die and knew he was beyond the help of any medical intervention. "It's your mom I'm worried about," the doctor concluded. "She is physically and emotionally depleted. You're going to have to do something."

When the doctor left the room, I battled a wave of discouragement clearly sent by the enemy of our soul. *How do you preach faith when your dad is lying here in this condition?* a voice jeered in my mind. *What do you tell people about God and healing and service? All of these years he was faithful, and now look how he has ended up!*

But as I stood at my father's bedside, God gave me the words from Scripture to win that struggle: "For we know that if the earthly tent which is our house is torn down, we have a building from God, a house not made with hands, eternal in the heavens" (2 Cor. 5:1 NASB).

"Devil," I said, "you're not going to win. When Dad closes his eyes in death, that old tabernacle, that tent, falls away. He's going to be in the presence of the King of kings and Lord of lords!"

When I stepped out of Dad's room, my mother was waiting. She asked what I had been doing. I said I had been praying for Dad. What she said next shocked me profoundly.

"Why are you praying for him?" she asked bitterly. "It won't do any good. Son, it's a joke." She poured out all her anguish over the previous years' prayers that appeared to be unanswered. "When you need God the most, He turns His back on you," she said. Then she pointed her finger in my face and said, "Son, don't you ever pray in my presence again."

As I drove home, reflecting on everything that had taken place, I began to cry. "God," I prayed, "if Dad passes, he will be in Your presence; but if something happens to Mom, she's lost her faith."

That night as I cried and worried over my mother's loss of faith, the Holy Spirit showed me the truth: She had not lost her faith at all. She had been trained and educated through decades of service to Christ in a faith that would never leave her. She knew in her mind the promises are true; but in her despair, she had lost hope.

The devil takes the only path he can. It is easier for the devil to discourage you emotionally than it is for him to defeat you scripturally. He can manipulate circumstances, but he cannot alter the Word of God. "For whatever was written in earlier times was written for our instruction, so that through perseverance and the encouragement of the Scriptures we might have hope" (Rom. 15:4 NASB).

Four days after my mother's angry, bitter, and hopeless outburst, she went back to the hospital to visit Dad. There, to her astonishment, she felt the presence of God.

"I didn't want to feel it," she told me later, "but it was like an anointing cloud."

In the Old Testament, they called it the Shekinah glory. God is so powerfully real. He has an essence about Him we can sometimes sense.

It was this essence of God's Spirit that came over my mother when she walked into Dad's room—and accompanying that essence, she heard a voice in her head. Four days earlier, the voice in my own head had been the Enemy trying to destroy my hope; but this day, it was the voice of the Holy Spirit whispering to my mother, *Get ready . . . he's going to talk to you today.*

That was crazy! The doctors had already told us Dad was "gone." Even if he came out of the coma, it had been months since he had spoken. His speech for three-and-a-half years leading up to this crisis had been unintelligible.

My mother had lost all hope, but now the voice of the Spirit was nudging her hope gauge just a little bit from "empty" to "full." She sat down by Dad's bed and waited with anticipation for what he would say.

"I don't know if I was there three minutes or three hours," she told me later, "but I was looking right into his eyes when they cleared up and he looked right at me. All of a sudden his mouth began to move, and with a strong voice he said, 'You know what, honey? God still answers prayer.'"

For the next ten minutes, my father lay there, praying in an unknown tongue under the power of the Holy Spirit. Finally, he slid back into the coma. He died soon afterward.

"Son, nobody else could have spoken that phrase to me," my mother declared afterward. "Not you, not any preacher, not any prophet—nobody could have spoken that phrase for it to have meant anything to me. The only man who could say that and it mean anything to me was your daddy—and he was brain-dead! But God let him preach one more message, and it restored my hope!"

When a pastor, sensitive to the voice of the Holy Spirit, steps behind a pulpit or onto a platform to communicate a message from the Word, it must ultimately be a message of hope. Pentecostal preaching that brings about discipleship growth is more than a review of scriptural truth, and more than a proclamation of the Spirit's empowerment and gifts; it is a wonderfully healing dose of hope that comes against the wounds inflicted by the Enemy.

Wounded disciples walk through the church doors every service. Unless we are listening to the Spirit and identifying with them in their pain, we cannot offer the guidance and encouragement that will carry them further in their God-directed paths, in their individual discipleship journeys. May each of us be sensitive to the Spirit's leading as we study the Word and prepare to deliver it to hungry and hurting hearts.

# 7
# Spirit-Filled Preaching Flows Out of a Spirit-Filled Life

### Hugh Bair

What is *Spirit-filled preaching*? Is Spirit-filled preaching different from other methods of Christian preaching? If so, are there a cluster of experiences that distinguish it from other traditions? The uniqueness of Spirit-filled preaching is that it is thoroughly rooted in the dynamic power of Pentecost. It flows from the same Spirit-filled life that was in full operation in the Book of Acts.

The generation of preachers represented in Acts made an astounding contribution to Spirit-filled preaching that we can use in the twenty-first century—a contribution that can guide preachers toward authentic spiritual practices. Spirit-filled preaching views sermon preparation from a devotional spiritual framework rather than a rhetorical, technical, homiletical task. It is directed toward keeping our hearts aligned with the Spirit of God.

Preaching is not just an art, a craft, or a moment in time between preacher and people; it is communication through the speaking of a consecrated personality who is on fire for God. Therefore, Spirit-filled preaching is based on our relationship with God and a quality of character that makes it inviting for Him to exercise His rule in the inner person. Additionally, character involves forthrightness in our relationship with God's people.

---

*Scriptures are from the King James Version.

Such preaching invites the spontaneous move of God, for it is grounded in prayer and a pure heart.

Preachers and students can benefit significantly from a Spirit-filled approach to preaching that fosters and maintains both spiritual and homiletic integrity. The task is to keep preachers faithful to the spiritual commission as set forth in the Bible.

The aim of this chapter is to broaden and deepen our current knowledge of preaching. This chapter will discuss four fundamentals to becoming an effective preacher in the twenty-first century:

1. Intimacy with God through consecrated prayer
2. Intimacy with God through devotional preparation
3. Intimacy with God through character development
4. Intimacy with God—a distinctive of Spirit-filled living

## Intimacy With God Through Consecrated Prayer

Prayer is speech addressed to God, and it is part of the sermon fabric that puts spiritual vitality into the sermon.[1] Let us consider Moses, the first one who was charged with the responsibility of delivering words from God to His chosen people. What unified and solidified Israel's relationship with God was the fact that Moses pitched his tent away from the rest of the camp in order to pray and have intimate dialogue with God. God came to meet with him, speaking face-to-face as a friend. As a result of this divine encounter, Moses gathered the people and told them what God had said. It is as close as we get in the Old Testament to the link between prayer and preaching that brings about a Spirit-filled transformational experience. It is safe to conclude that the origin of preaching may have emerged out of a prayer dialogue between a preacher and God, but its effectiveness was manifested when the children of Israel took hold of the Word and went to the Red Sea to see the deliverance of God.

In the New Testament, prayer is indispensable and becomes the background for ministry. In Paul's epistles, in order to function as a leader, one was urged to make prayer an essential part of his or her life. Therefore, prayer in the context of ministry is the foundation for a preacher's spiritual life, and that produces a deep Spirit-filled life.[2] Raewynne Whiteley wrote:

> Lancelot Andrewes, the great seventeenth-century bishop, preacher, and translator of the King James Version of the Bible, is said to have spent five hours per day in prayer; 150 years later, John Wesley prayed for a minimum of two hours.[3]

Paul's letters reveal he experienced vital spirituality that was inspired by the Holy Spirit. For example, not only did Paul have an intimate relationship with the Holy Spirit (Rom. 8:26), but his Spirit-filled prayer had a sanctifying effect (1 Tim. 4:5) that gave authority to his preaching as well. The power of Paul's preaching flowed out of a Spirit-filled life. I am convinced that the power of one's preaching is predicated on or established through the preacher's acute intimate relationship with Christ as he or she practices the disciplines of prayer. Paul wrote under the unction of the Spirit to the Ephesian church:

> [Pray] for me, that utterance may be given unto me, that I may open my mouth boldly, to make known the mystery of the gospel, for which I am an ambassador in bonds: that therein I may speak boldly, as I ought to speak (6:19-20).

As we give serious attention to the interpretation of the biblical text in order to gain a greater understanding of the meaning of contextuality in proclamation, we can see Paul emphasized a connection between prayer and homiletics in his writing. Furthermore, we can tell that this connection meant a lot to him because he repeated the same approach in Colossians:

> Withal praying also for us, that God would open unto us a door of utterance, to speak the mystery of Christ, for which I

am also in bonds: that I may make it manifest, as I ought to speak (4:3-4).

In both of the above-cited passages, Paul was soliciting prayer for his preaching ministry. In Ephesians, Paul is concerned about the *content* of his preaching, desiring to communicate the right words. However, in Colossians, Paul is soliciting prayer to support the *style* of his preaching. In both of these scriptures, Paul wants the style and content of his preaching to be soaked in prayer that would produce Spirit-filled preaching.

Praying in the Spirit is a spiritual practice. As a discipline, the act of praying in the Spirit has the potential or the ability of positioning the Pentecostal/Charismatic preacher in a place where the Holy Spirit can go about the process of transformation and personal edification.

The Pentecostal practice of speaking in tongues, which is technically called *glossolalia*, often manifests itself as praying in tongues.[4] Praying in tongues, as a discipline of prayer, functions as a Pentecostal spiritual practice by allowing a Pentecostal/Charismatic preacher or pastor to create an environment whereby the Holy Spirit can continually transform him or her into the image of Christ. Habitual praying in tongues feeds the preaching process in unexpected ways. For example, the Holy Spirit has the ability to enrich one's vocabulary and echo the power of God in the life of the congregation. In short, glossolalia is a linguistic symbol of the sacred. So, for the Pentecostal/Charismatic preacher, it is a precious possession, a divine gift.[5]

The contemporary crisis in the Pentecostal/Charismatic Movement and the Christian church at large has been caused by a disconnect between doing and being, technique and spirituality. The problem is about pragmatic technique that has tended to divorce prayer from homiletics. Such a dynamic brings the power to *do* but not the power to *be*. It produces preachers that lack the foundation from which ministry flows—a heart that has been transformed and remade into the image of Christ by the power of prayer.

This foundation is a missing part of Pentecostal spirituality, although it was an integral part of the historical development of the Pentecostal doctrine. The Pentecostal church has received the "chalice" of preaching. This is the gift of proclamation that was demonstrated in the Book of Acts (2:47). Before the Day of Pentecost, only 120 were gathered in an upper room; then, on the Day of Pentecost, 3,000 people were convicted and turned to the Lord.

A *chalice* is a silver cup containing wine. The dynamic of Pentecost is that the church received the wine of the Spirit. As the church drank the sweet wine of the Spirit, it loosed their tongues and lubricated their lips; and they proclaimed the dynamic of Pentecost. They were "people of the chalice."

The time in which we live embraces a de-emphasis on preaching which plagues seminaries and churches. I believe part of the process of Spirit-filled preaching is to reclaim the chalice of the Spirit given on the Day of Pentecost. Nevertheless, one's effectiveness as a preacher or pastor will depend on his or her ability to pray. This is a great resource that must be guarded.[6] One of the potential dangers for the preacher is to become too busy and never take time to speak with God. It is much easier to be accountable for deadlines that must be checked off than the number of hours spent in intimate communion with God through prayer. But spending time with God is essential for our lives as preachers.[7]

The beginning of my sermon is prefaced with prayer, as I speak to God and ask Him to speak to me. I believe every sermon I preach must be dictated, directed, and delivered by the Holy Spirit; otherwise, it is not a sermon. Therefore, praying before writing is the only way I can come within hearing range of a conversation to find out what God wants to say to Christian Life Church. I have discovered that praying has sustained my preaching, fed my soul, and opened me up to experiences that I would never have known otherwise.

While I am preparing a sermon, I always pray for the hearers—that the Spirit will make their hearts fertile ground for the good seed of God's Word. The real preacher is the Holy Spirit. Unless the Spirit preaches, no preaching happens. One cannot preach without praying. It is the Holy Spirit who really preaches through the preacher to convict, convince, and convert those who hear about what God has done.

Scripture often refers to fasting in combination with prayer. *Fasting* refers to abstaining from food for intentional reasons to increase spirituality. Richard Foster stated the following about fasting:

> The list of biblical personages who fasted becomes a "Who's Who" of Scripture: Moses the lawgiver, David the king, Elijah the prophet, Esther the queen, Daniel the seer, Anna the prophetess, Paul the apostle, Jesus Christ the incarnate Son. Many of the great Christians through church history fasted and witnessed to its value; among them were Martin Luther, John Calvin, John Knox, John Wesley, Jonathan Edwards, David Brainerd, Charles Finney, and Pastor Hsi of China.[8]

One of the benefits of fasting for the preacher is that it opens up the opportunity to intentionally seek God's will and grace in a way that goes beyond the normal habitats of sermon preparation. While fasting, we are one with God in an intimate relationship, offering Him the time and attentiveness we might otherwise be giving to eating.[9] My mother was a powerful Pentecostal/Charismatic woman of God who operated in the gifts of the Spirit and who taught me the spiritual disciplines of fasting and "praying through."

"Praying through" happens to a child of God when he or she feels in their spirit that God has answered their prayer. And it has been the power of fasting that has sustained my preaching ministry and has prevented it from being boring, uninteresting, irrelevant, and uninspiring. I do some of my most creative writing and sermon preparation while fasting. A person's mental functioning usually improves as his or her body cleans, repairs, and rejuvenates. The scientific world of psychology has suggested that through the power of fasting a person can increase concentration and broadening of the mind.[10] It is when the heart and the mind of the preacher are touched by God that the sermon becomes compelling and can transform the lives of listeners. Ray H. Hughes Sr. said, "Fasting is a must for Pentecostal preaching. It entreats God's presence, it sensitizes the soul, and it prepares the preacher to follow the direction of the spirit."[11]

In Mark 9, the disciples were impotent, powerless, and irrelevant because of their lack of fasting and praying. Fasting reminds us that we need to feed our souls, for the responsibility of the preacher is spiritual feeding and attending to the nourishment of the souls of God's people.

## Intimacy With God Through Devotional Preparation

A person's devotional life will determine the true height and depth of his or her preaching ministry. *Devotion* means "consecration," "dedication," and "zeal."[12] A preacher's devotional life should be the number one priority. It is the main springboard of all effective service, for it makes the difference between knowing about God and actually knowing Him.

Daily devotion would not be considered essential in some academic situations, but I suggest to young preachers and pastors that not doing daily devotions is to pass over not only the power to preach but even something to preach. Devotions have a powerful effect on sermon preparation and delivery. To neglect the discipline of daily devotions is to neglect the essence of preaching: power, preparation, and proclamation. It is by the process of daily devotion that God reveals what He wants His proclaimers to preach. So, succinctly, my first approach to sermon preparation is daily devotion.

In the midst of a very busy life with so many demands on his or her time, a preacher must fence off a definite time when he or she can pray and do devotional reading of Scripture. Just as intimacy with one's spouse must be deliberate, so too must intimacy with God be by design. This is not something a preacher does automatically; it requires determination, commitment, and discipline. A preacher or pastor's devotional time must be constantly and jealously guarded, lest step-by-step it is gradually eroded by other duties, pushed into a corner, and finally loses its value completely.

Spiritual intimacy lending itself to Spirit-filled devotional disciplines of sermon preparation involves a fourfold process of Scripture reading, meditating/waiting, travailing, and praying in tongues.

## 1. Scripture Reading

Spirit-filled preaching is centered on the Word of God. Therefore, I must saturate myself with Scripture. As I soak myself in the Bible, I am nourished by what it says. The psalmist said, "Thy word have I hid in mine heart" (119:11).

Every time I reached for my Bible and read it, I was looking for a sermon. If I was not careful, Saturday would sneak up on me with rhythmic-like predictability, and I would have to develop a sermon. This approach is physically demanding and emotionally frustrating. The better way for me has been a devotional approach. In other words, I put myself in a prayerful situation so the text will "find" me. Once the Holy Spirit has "found" the text, I want Him to speak to my heart. I have learned to ask, "Lord, what are You saying to me in the text? What is the relevance of this passage for the present age in which I live? What needs to be communicated from this word to the people whom I pastor?" But before I can get the answer to these questions, I find it necessary to exegete myself. In other words, I honestly confront myself in light of the Word of God. I like to read a Scripture passage slowly and out loud, lingering over the words so they resonate in my heart. I do not read the words for psychological analysis of the text or for information; rather, it is reading for reception—an attentive listening to what the Holy Spirit of God is saying.

## 2. Meditating/Waiting

Spirit-filled preaching involves a process of meditating and waiting before the Lord. Acts 1:4 states, "They should not depart from Jerusalem, but wait for the promise of the Father." Read the Scripture, then wait and meditate on it. It is your daily food; and if you don't have that daily food, you are like a withered flower. It is nourishment to the soul. It is being present in the moment with God. Reflect on the importance of God's words. Gardner Taylor says we must walk up and down the "street" of the text.[13] We center on the text, allowing it to soak deep into our souls and asking God to drench us in it. I find it interesting that the Spirit of the Lord God "moved" ("brooded" or "hovered") over the water in Creation (Gen. 1:2). When this happens in our environment, many things come to our cognitive mind that will be richly rewarding for pulpit work.

At this point, you enter into a personal conversation with God. In other words, as you meditate and wait on God, you will discover the Living Word of God has the capacity to directly and immediately address our own maladaptive issues and the contemporary times in which we live.[14]

## 3. Travailing

Spirit-filled preaching can possibly involve a process of groaning or travailing before God that can be painful. By travailing, one who is about to preach demonstrates his or her dependency on God. Romans 8:26 states, "We know not what we should pray for as we ought: but the Spirit itself maketh intercession for us with groanings which cannot be uttered." The Holy Spirit prays with us according to the will of God. The groanings of the Spirit are inarticulate, but God receives these groanings as acceptable prayers inasmuch as they come from a preacher whose soul is full of the Holy Spirit.

Preaching is physically demanding, and it can be emotionally frustrating trying to find out what to preach. As stated previously, Sunday always comes with rhythmic-like predictability, and that is why we need the Holy Spirit to help us find the mind and the will of God so we can speak with authority. There are times when I do not know what to preach, but the Holy Spirit makes intercession for me with groanings, and then the Spirit becomes the interpreter of my groanings. In other words, He takes my twisted words and straightens them out, making intercession for me so I will have God's message for His people. The more I wrestle for the right word in my devotions, the more power I gain to preach.

## 4. Praying in Tongues

Pentecostals believe that speaking in tongues is the initial evidence of baptism in the Holy Spirit. In other words, this remarkable manifestation is just what it says it is—the audible or vocalized sign that one is filled with the Spirit of God. A word of caution needs to be emphasized here, however: the devotional aspect of speaking in tongues is not self-initiated—it only takes place when the Spirit gives utterance to the preacher. The experience can only be encountered by one who is yielded to the power of God.

Therefore, Spirit-filled preaching can also involve speaking in tongues, should the Spirit lead that way. At this point, you begin to enter into a personal conversation with God. In other words, you give voice to what is happening in your soul. It is the place of spontaneous utterances when you respond truthfully and authentically. B. E. Underwood discusses *devotional tongues*.[15] Devotional tongues are given to the believer to aid him or her in worship to God. These are scriptural underpinnings to support the spiritual premises for praying in tongues, praising in tongues, singing in tongues, and interceding in tongues. Paul writes, "What is it then? I will pray with the spirit, and I will pray with the understanding also: I will sing with the spirit, and I will sing with the understanding also" (1 Cor. 14:15).

It is important to identify another dimension of empowerment that comes about when one is involved in praying in the Spirit. When one is praying according to the mind of the Holy Spirit, his or her praying comes into perfect agreement with what God desires to say to His people. According to Bishop James Forbes, "Part of the sermon preparation process is that you have to know what the Lord is saying to *you* about what the people are saying."[16] Praying in tongues takes us to a dimension in the Spirit that enables us to communicate through the mouth that God has put in our spirit when we may not have the cognitive resources to do it. This dimension of the Spirit takes us into deeper growth and broader frontiers in our preaching.

Individuals or preachers who claim they are filled with the Spirit do not make a psychological or spiritual assessment that they are deeper in God. Steven Land wrote:

> Those who are filled with the Spirit have no inherent claim to superiority that can be sustained by the Scriptures. However, they all testify to walking in the light that God has shined on their paths. They all testify to the fact that their Christian lives are better and stronger and that they are more effective in their witness than they were before.[17]

Sometimes the Spirit of God works in me with a soft but insistent voice, giving me the idea as to what needs to be said in the sermon so the people of God will be nourished or built up. Or, sometimes I am led by the Spirit to Wesley Theological Seminary in Washington, D.C., to research a topic. Some of my best moments I have experienced in preaching were not in the pulpit before the people, but having the Spirit guiding me as I prepare to preach. There are times when I have to stand up and walk around because the Word is like fire in my bones. Spirit-filled preaching flows out of a Spirit-filled life that is shaped through the uniqueness of one's devotional life. When that process takes place, we shift from devotion to delivery of the sermon.

The crucial question for a preacher or pastor to ask is, Do I have a personal relationship with God, or am I totally defined by the ministry I carry out to others? The tendency for many pastors is often an unhealthy neglect of self and a compulsive caretaking of others.[18] Therefore, we must realize that if we do not control our calendars, they will control us, so it becomes necessary to schedule daily devotional time.

There are rewards that come with a disciplined life. For example, it is during our personal devotional time that, as pastors or preachers, we sustain our ministries and our identities. As we connect with God on an interpersonal level, there is a spiritual deepening into the things of God—praise, thanksgiving, repentance, petition, intercession, and prayer.[19] Prayer awakens the soul and opens doors of possibility. Prayer is the liberation of that inner voice of the external that we as pastors need to guide us. At heart, prayer is a devotional process of self-giving and of being set free from feelings of being in isolation in the ministry. To pray is to enter into a relationship with God and to be transformed by Him. This devotional prayer with God results in emotional and spiritual renewal, social responsiveness, joy, gratitude, acceptance of one's losses, loyalty to God, perseverance, and integration of the personality. In other words, our devotional life feeds us spiritually.

## Intimacy With God Through Character Development

Think about the following questions:
1. Does the spiritual quality or lifestyle of a preacher determine the message that he or she delivers?

2. How does character as manifested in the sermon contribute to the process of proclamation, and does it have an impact on the congregation?
3. What is the relationship between character and preaching that makes Spirit-filled preaching different from other existing traditions?

The interrelationship between the pastor or preacher's life and his character matters to God. We are to be "examples to the flock" (see 1 Peter 5:3).[20] The partnership or congruity between the pastor or preacher's life and his character was expressed well by Fred Craddock:

> The message and the messenger are experienced together by the listeners. . . . The person of the preacher can be an asset or a liability, even a contradiction, to the preaching event. Therefore, the person as well as the sermon is prepared.[21]

It is in the process of being filled with the Spirit of God that the Holy Spirit probes the preacher, giving him or her insight into the felt needs of the congregation.

Authentic character cannot be hidden or masked. Character oozes out of us while we are in the process of proclamation. We constantly give people insight into the psychological interior construct of our personality as we engage in preaching the Word. For example, personality problems can have a negative impact on preaching, such as a narcissistic attention to one's self, mannerisms, and opinions, or frequent airing of personal affronts and grievances, stubbornness, and self-indulgent excuses for not being prepared.

As one who worked as a resident in clinical psychology and who practiced psychotherapy with clients at Christian Psychotherapy Services in Virginia, I discovered there are preachers who clearly meet the diagnostic criteria for narcissistic personality disorder. There are individuals with narcissistic behavior who are drawn to the ministry. This could be because of the high visibility and the opportunity to be in a position of leadership. Nevertheless, one's personality cannot be eliminated or excused from preaching, for personality is a *means* that the Holy Spirit will use as an instrument through which the good news is delivered.

The inside of the preacher is always on display; therefore, self-disclosure is always part of the preaching process. People intuitively sense more about us than they can prove by the way we present ourselves to them. We become known through our psychological and emotional manner and the way we communicate, verbally and nonverbally.[22] Character involves integrity and forthrightness in our relationship with God's people. Character is a display of our personality that has continuity over time. Integrity means being consistent in our behavior. Our character protects us from scandals.[23]

According to Ray Corsini, *integrity* is "completeness of structure; an unimpaired condition; the quality of moral consistency, honesty, and truthfulness."[24] When preachers live without integrity of character, they may try to promote a worthwhile cause, yet they will fail to gain a following because their lives discredit the validity of who they are. Sometimes the preacher who has no integrity is viewed as a finger-licking, chicken-eating, womanizing, money-grabbing swindler who has no ethics and who will use the pulpit to exploit a congregation.

I served as senior pastor for Springfield Church of God for thirteen years. If I were to return to that church for a visit, it is unlikely the people would remember the sermons I preached. They might remember an illustration or a time when I was there for them in a time of crisis. The congregation at Springfield would not remember how well I crafted a sermon with explanation, illustration, application, and Pentecostal celebration. What they would remember is that during the time I was there, the words I preached were consistent with my character. In other words, what people need from a pastor is that his or her tongue and behavior are in complete unity. People are more inclined to believe preachers whose words are coherent with their characters.[25]

Since our character and personality have a dynamic impact on the sermon and its credibility, we are called upon to "practice what we preach."[26] Our character and integrity determine the power of the sermon more than how well the sermon is crafted. If we are going to preach a sermon that flows out of a Spirit-filled life and emphasizes the centrality of the Spirit's presence, we must be vertically connected to God in a spiritual way and horizontally connected to our congregation.

The early church father Augustine listed three essential tools in communication: *logos*, *pathos*, and *ethos*. *Logos* is the ability to connect with the mind. There should be something in the sermon that is logical in its presentation. *Pathos* refers to the emotions—to the arousal of feelings of pity, sympathy, tenderness, or sorrow. Listeners should feel something while the preacher is preaching. They should be deeply moved by what is said. *Ethos* is the more essential critical component in communication. It is the character of the Spirit-filled preacher. People are not just listening to a message; they are listening to a person. So, the "who" of the preacher affects people's listening more than "what" is actually being said.[27] The preacher is not to be thought of as simply a holy kind of conduit by which the Word is conveyed like water through a pipe.

John Wesley was known more for his ethos than his homiletical skills or his eloquence. Wesley had something working in his favor that gave him incredible power in his preaching—it was his character—and when he spoke, the power of God oozed from him. Clearly, Wesley walked before God in an intimate way. And his personal ethos made up for his lack of rhetorical ability.[28]

The main power of preaching comes out of a disciplined spirituality. The visible power that is felt in the pulpit is not born of rhetorical cleverness or skill but of a relationship with God.

## Intimacy With God—A Distinctive of Spirit-Filled Living

Spirit-filled preaching is a distinctive of a Spirit-filled life. It is based on one's character or integrity; and it is punctuated with the supernatural, the extraordinary, and the unexpected. More often than not, power is the result of purity of heart before the Lord—as He will trust a servant with power who is given to holiness. That is to say, power most often will not bring purity of heart, while a pure heart will move God to entrust someone with power. Ray H. Hughes said:

> In the pulpit, under the anointing of God's Spirit, men often speak and act beyond themselves. There are times when a word of knowledge, a word of wisdom, or a revelation comes to the preacher right out of heaven.[29]

The supernatural working of the Spirit in the character of the preacher comes with abandonment or "letting go"—the self yielding to the Spirit. This dynamic process happens when the preacher or pastor lives a consistent lifestyle that is absolutely dependent on God.

A characteristic that makes Spirit-filled preaching distinctive is that it invites the spontaneous and the immediate. The spontaneity involved in the delivery of the sermon is based on what God is performing internally in the character of the pastor or preacher. Ethos is character, and it is spiritually derived and cultivated by a relationship with God. Sometimes a preacher might not have the education or oratorical skills that he or she might desire. But because of his or her sincere character, God is able to transmit a message. In other words, no matter how unpolished the sermon is, people are drawn to God by the preaching because the minister is kind and loving, and God's Spirit is working in him or her.

Spirit-filled preaching flows out of a Spirit-filled life that is fostering ethos, and it breaks through in the pulpit. This flooding in of the Spirit of God is manifested in an external way. For example, during the worship service, the Spirit might manifest Himself in the preacher's mind with sudden inspiration or creative ability. This creative ability appeals to kinesthetic (hands-on) learners. Kinesthetic learners want to be drawn into what the Spirit of God is doing by participating in a physical way.[30]

For example, the Holy Spirit will sometimes use the Spirit-filled preacher to engage the people in the sermon by getting them to raise their hands in worship, shake hands with another worshiper, or do a brief drama on the platform in order to illustrate what needs to be said to sustain attention. At times, I have performed a skit on the platform by using people in the congregation. The skit is unexpected, unplanned, and unrehearsed, and comes in a creative way as I am moved by the Spirit of God—for I have learned that creativity flourishes when the Spirit is moving. This homiletical skill comes from God to improve the communication of the gospel to those who find it difficult to hear. Therefore, Spirit-filled preaching makes ample use of both illustration and exposition, and it is not afraid to take a risk.

Another distinctive of Spirit-filled preaching is its necessity to adapt to the personality of the preacher. In the nineteenth century, the outstanding preacher Phillips Brooks defined *preaching* as "truth through personality."[31] In other words, Brooks believed God never sets aside the essential features of the preacher's personality. Preaching can be understood as the vocalization of a character. It is a life that is speaking. It is a supernatural act of God using a person to convey the everlasting Jesus.

In Spirit-filled preaching, the human personality is sanctified by the Spirit of God. To be *sanctified* is to be "set apart" for God's purpose by the Holy Spirit.[32] The sanctified preacher ought to preach out of his or her "dedication," "consecration," or "holiness." If the preacher ceases to develop spiritually, his or her preaching will also cease to develop, for the work of preaching is born of *being* the message. Spirit-filled preaching flows out of a Spirit-filled life that is sanctified before God. One's sanctification bears witness that he or she is genuine and credible to the congregation. As the preacher submits to the Holy Spirit, the Word of God is constantly flooding the heart and the mind, and, as a result, we can tell others to drink of this living water because they will be able to detect that we are also drinking from it.

Another feature of Spirit-filled preaching that can be manifested in the character of the preacher is its authority. Anchored in the Word of God, it exhibits the dynamic power of the Spirit in worship. Spirit-filled preaching is centered on the Scriptures and is, therefore, directed and empowered by the Holy Spirit. In the Book of Acts, we see the early church was Christ-centered and Word-dominated. All of the members were involved in proclaiming the Word, and the Word of God was the foundation of all preaching. The church was shaped by the Word of God. In order for the contemporary church to maintain its power of vitality and its purposeful existence, the Word of God must be the overarching, penetrating, piercing theme.

When the Word of God is being preached, there will be power in the pulpit and the pew; in other words, there will be a response from the congregation. As the preacher is full to overflowing with the Word, the congregation gets involved. It is like the preacher and the congregation are spiritually feeding one another. Or, it is as if they are metaphorically dancing together in the Spirit.

If the people do not say "Amen" or give other passionate response, it usually means the Spirit has decided not to speak through the preacher at that time. Whatever psychological observation one might try to make, the absence of a "Hallelujah" and "Praise the Lord" when the preacher or pastor speaks God's Word is uncharacteristic of Spirit-filled preaching. The responses let the preacher know that he or she is moving in the right direction, as what is being said rings true to the Spirit's presence in their midst.

## Spirit-Filled Preaching Flows Out of a Spirit-Filled Life

There is no understanding of Spirit-filled preaching flowing out of a Spirit-filled life apart from the presence of the Spirit, who descends upon the gathered community as the Word of God is being preached. Radical transformation by the power of the Spirit is the hallmark of Spirit-filled preaching as the anointing flows out of the life of the preacher. When that happens, it is an electrifying event. Spirit-filled preaching is not only an external manifestation but also internal work in the life of the minister.

The Word of God is preached through human beings. God is a personal being who usually comes to people through other people. The most profound coming of God was through the incarnation of Jesus. The "Word" of God came through the flesh of Mary. The concept of the Incarnation is powerful and dynamic. However, I am convinced we need to make it more pragmatic in our understanding that Spirit-filled preaching flows out of a Spirit-filled life.

The Incarnation meant Mary went through many hours of body-stretching labor that involved moaning and groaning to relieve the pain.[33] Incarnational preaching means that the preacher spends many hours in preparation so the Spirit of God can embody the Word of life into his or her spirit. James Earl Massey called it "a burdensome joy."[34] Those of us who preach frequently understand that sermons come by effort and anguish as one tarries or groans in the Spirit in order to hear from God. His Word comes both from the outside of us as Scripture, and takes up dwelling in us so that at the appointed time the Spirit-birthed Word can come forth. Once the Word is birthed or delivered out of the character or personality of the preacher or pastor, there is inspired joy in the minds of those who listen. The preacher's character and the work of the Spirit give direction and shape, form, cooperativeness, and purposefulness to the preached Word.[35] The Spirit-filled preacher is oriented to the life and work of the Spirit as he or she works in collaboration and agreeability with God.

Spirit-filled preaching flows out of a Spirit-filled life that is rooted in the dynamic power of Pentecost. This dynamic power flows from a preacher who leads a consecrated devotional life that is soaked in the spiritual discipline of prayer, which is a pivotal component for sermon preparation. The power in preaching comes not from one's rhetorical cleverness or oratory skill, but from a relationship with God. Ministry in general is an extension of our relationship with God—and in the case of Spirit-filled preaching, Spirit-filled living is an essential.

If preaching is to be understood as a spiritual practice, then more needs to be said about the ways in which preachers can become proficient in that spiritual practice in the twenty-first century. I believe Spirit-filled preaching that is saturated in Pentecostal power is the answer for this age. Such anointed proclamation is born of no less than intimacy with God and purity of heart—a holy heart with no rivals that is set apart to love God supremely. We can turn the spiritual atmosphere around with Spirit-possessed preachers—men and women filled to overflowing with God himself. Preachers will be immediately recognizable by the power of their speech because they have been in the presence of God, and the presence of God abides in them.

To be sure, Spirit-filled preaching flows out of a Spirit-filled life. My prayer is that the Holy Spirit will use this chapter to start a new work in your life and that you will bring transformation and fresh fire to your community.

# 8

# How to Prepare and Preach Expository Sermons

### John A. Lombard Jr.

The Bible is restored to its place of authority. Every need in the intergenerational, multicultural audience can be addressed. The mandate "Preach the Word" (2 Tim. 4:2) is heeded. The awesome challenge to be God's spokesperson for reconciliation can be fulfilled. The people of God can be discipled, equipped, and matured through God's Word. God's revelation is communicated in words and ideas understood so that the purpose of preaching is accomplished—the transformation of human lives! These are some of the benefits of expository preaching.

## Expository Preaching Acknowledges the Power of God's Word

### God's Word Is the Route to Faith

"Faith comes from hearing the message, and the message is heard through the word of Christ" (Rom. 10:17). The preaching of the Word of God brings faith into the heart and increases faith. When people seem faithless, keep preaching the Word.

In Jesus' account of the rich man and Lazarus (Luke 16:19-31), the rich man requested that Lazarus be sent back to earth to

*Scriptures are from the *New International Version* unless otherwise indicated.

warn his five brothers. "Abraham replied, 'They have Moses and the Prophets; let them listen to them.' But he said, 'No, Father Abraham,' he said, 'but if someone from the dead goes to them, they will repent.' He said to him, 'If they do not listen to Moses and the Prophets, they will not be convinced even if someone rises from the dead'" (vv. 29-31).

If the Scriptures are not sufficient to generate faith, nothing will.

### God's Word Is the Agent of His Transforming Power

"For I am not ashamed of the gospel of Christ, for it is the power of God to salvation for everyone who believes" (Rom. 1:16 NKJV). The Romans depended on military power, and the preaching of a crucified Christ seemed weakness. Paul said, however, that the *gospel*— "the good news of Christ"—is God's power demonstrated. "When you received the word of God, which you heard from us, you accepted it not as the word of men, but as it actually is, the word of God, which is at work in you who believe" (1 Thess. 2:13).

### God's Word Is the Demonstration of His Power

Paul said Christ sent him "to preach the gospel [evangelize]—not with words of human wisdom, lest the cross of Christ be emptied of its power. For the message of the cross is foolishness to those who are perishing, but to us who are being saved it is the power of God" (1 Cor. 1:17-18).

### God's Word Softens and Purifies Hard Hearts

"'Let the one who has my word speak it faithfully. . . . Is not my word like a fire,'" declares the Lord, "and like a hammer that breaks a rock in pieces?" (Jer. 23:28-29). Diplomacy may fail . . . counseling may fail . . . other human efforts may fail; but keep on preaching God's Word. Allow His Word the opportunity to break through the barriers and overcome the obstacles.

## God's Word Brings Understanding and Openness to the Abundance of His Provision

"While Peter was still speaking these words, the Holy Spirit came on all who heard the message" (Acts 10:44). As the Holy Spirit brought understanding about God's provision, He also brought openness of heart to receive from God. The preacher needs to expect God to be at work through the preaching of the Word. God desires to work through every preaching opportunity. No preaching opportunity should be looked at as a routine event, because God is at work!

Acknowledging the power of God's Word, the expositor seeks to proclaim God's Word. *Expository preaching* is expounding the truths from a passage of Scripture under a central idea arising from the text studied—in its historical, theological, and literary contexts—and applied to the speaker and hearers. From this definition, one can see that an expository sermon does not come from a superficial reading of a text. It does not come from a preacher's deciding what to preach and then finding a text that seems to substantiate the idea. It is not stringing together verses from a concordance without considering their contexts. It is not downloading and delivering someone else's sermon, thereby becoming a mimic and not the unique spokesperson for God that He intended. Expository preaching is an exciting and challenging venture that will bring spiritual growth to the preacher and multiplied dividends to the hearers.

How can a preacher decide what to say without really knowing what God is saying? Knowing what God is saying does not merely depend on what others have said, but it depends upon prayerfully studying God's Word. Ezra's example is worthwhile: "Ezra had set his heart to study the law of the Lord, and to do it, and to teach the statutes and ordinances in Israel" (7:10 NRSV). Study, practice, and proclaim. Paul told Timothy, "Do your best to present yourself to God as one approved by him, a worker who has no need to be ashamed, rightly explaining the word of truth" (2 Tim. 2:15 NRSV). The preacher is confident that the Holy Spirit will anoint and guide in the study so the truth is understood: "When he, the Spirit of truth, comes, he will guide you into all truth" (John 16:13).

## Understanding the Text

The first emphasis of expository preaching is *understanding* the selected passage of Scripture. Whatever the initial thought which guided one to the passage, the Word of God must be the foundation and source of the sermon. What was God saying to the original hearers? In order to ascertain an answer to that question, the expositor first gives attention to the *historical context*: Who was the human author? What was his relationship to the recipients? What were some of their challenges, needs, and problems? What was the author's purpose in writing the book? When was the book written? For example, for an Old Testament prophet, was it written prior to the Assyrian invasion, or prior to the Babylonian invasion?

It is important to observe the *type of literature* which the passage is in, and to explore various interpretive principles related to that type. Among the forms of biblical literature are poetry, narrative, prophecy, wisdom, apocalyptic, Gospels, and Epistles. In poetry, give attention to figurative language.

- In narrative, note the lessons and principles.
- In prophecy, the prophet generally spoke in prosperous times to call the people back to God, so know their times and the message to the original hearers.
- In wisdom literature, the theological perspective of the speaker is important.
- Apocalyptic literature was generally spoken/written during difficult days to comfort the people of God.
- The Gospels are "good news" about Jesus Christ.

- God guided the writers of the Epistles, or letters, to enlarge our theological base and to show how Christian theology is lived out in the world.

One of the most important considerations in preparing an expository sermon is the *literary context*—the biblical material that surrounds the text. The immediate context consists of the verses prior to and the verses after the text. There is usually a flow of meaning in this extended material. The context expands to include the section of the book, the Old or New Testament, and the entire Bible. If the text seems to contradict any of its contexts, another understanding needs to be explored. In a narrative passage, the longer story needs to be read in order to better understand the smaller part. For example, in noting Samuel's not knowing the voice of the Lord (1 Sam. 3), it is helpful to know that the Word of the Lord was rare in those days; the priesthood was corrupt; Eli had neglected to discipline his sons; and the child Samuel had been left by his mother, Hannah, to serve in the Temple under the tutelage of Eli.

The expositor depends on the Holy Spirit to superintend *analyzing the text*. Read the passage in several translations and write down all the thoughts you have arising from the text. Refrain from reading what others think until you have discerned what the text is saying. Refrain from cross-referencing until you have thought deeply about the passage before you. At this point, it is helpful to do further research in commentaries, Bible dictionaries, word studies, and so forth. Be alert to the background and bias of the author of each commentary. Compare and contrast the various views, and pray that the Holy Spirit will guide you in discerning the truth.

Let's see how these principles work in practice by prayerfully considering Matthew 6:1, 5-8.

> "Beware of practicing your piety before others in order to be seen by them; for then you have no reward from your Father in heaven. . . . And whenever you pray, do not be like the hypocrites; for they love to stand and pray in the synagogues

and at the street corners, so that they may be seen by others. Truly I tell you, they have received their reward. But whenever you pray, go into your room and shut the door and pray to your Father who is in secret; and your Father who sees in secret will reward you. When you are praying, do not heap up empty phrases as the Gentiles do; for they think that they will be heard because of their many words. Do not be like them, for your Father knows what you need before you ask him" (NRSV).

Briefly, the historical context consists of Matthew's writing primarily to Jewish believers to show how Jesus fulfills the Old Testament prophecies concerning the Messiah. The genealogy of Jesus emphasizes Jesus as "the son of David, the son of Abraham" (1:1), while Luke, with a Gentile audience, shows Jesus' genealogy as going back to "the son of Adam, the son of God" (3:38). The material of Matthew was probably first circulated in the last part of the first century.

Our passage is from a synoptic Gospel, specifically from a teaching of Jesus to His disciples, known as "The Sermon on the Mount." Our text is in the section dealing with giving, praying, and fasting. Matthew 6:1 is the caption of this whole section. In the passage prior to verses 5-8, Jesus gives instructions concerning giving, and in the verses after, He gives instructions concerning fasting.

Before you read any further comments about the passage, I urge you to pause and write down everything that comes to mind as you prayerfully read through it several times. Please note now some thoughts, which probably already occurred to you.

Jesus gave a stern warning about practicing deeds of righteousness, piety, or spiritual disciplines with impure motives. With impure motive, our prayers are not answered by the Father. Jesus begins with negatives and moves to positives. Jesus said, "*When* you pray." He did not say, "*If* you pray." Prayer is expected of a disciple.

The hypocrites received their reward from the accolades of others, not from God. The believer's prayers are to be different;

they are not just spontaneous, but planned, deliberate, an appointment with God—"go into your room, shut the door, pray to your Father." The Father promises to reward. Our prayers are not like the pagans who try to impress their gods by many words; we just talk to God with plain speech. We pray to the Father with confidence that He already knows our need even before we ask. That is comforting because sometimes we see only the symptoms and God alone knows the need.

These are just thoughts arising out of this passage. There are enough truths here from Jesus about prayer without our including any other verses in the sermon. Apparently Jesus thought the instructions to be sufficient at that point.

You can discover other insights with further research. You could explore the word *hypocrite*—it refers to speaking from behind a mask, the approach of the actors of that time. You could discover that homes of that era had one room with a door—their treasure room. Bills of sale were discovered with the word translated "have their reward" (meaning "paid in full") written across them.

## Determining the Approach

When the expositor is confident that the truth of the text has been discovered, the next step is to determine the *approach*—the shape or the structure of the sermon. The expository sermon is not a verse by verse commentary; this would be laborious, dull, and boring. In most cases it should not include the historical context which enlightened you, but would bog the sermon down. Only parts of it which are necessary for understanding should be shared.

The distinctiveness of the expository sermon is not necessarily in the shape or structure but in the in-depth study and the proclamation of those truths from the Word of God. The expositor seeks to understand God's message in the text, apply it to himself/herself, and then to find the best way for the message to be communicated to the hearers. The variety of approaches would include *deductive, inductive, narrative,* and *first-person.* Most expository sermons follow the deductive approach, which we will explore now.

In the *deductive approach,* the text is read and then expounded. In synagogue worship, the rabbi stood and read the text, and then sat down to expound it. Luke 4 records Jesus' ministry in the synagogue in Nazareth. He stood and read from the scroll of Isaiah and then sat down and shared with them the ultimate meaning of Isaiah's message.

The early church followed the deductive approach primarily. The sermon by Simon Peter on the Day of Pentecost (Acts 2) begins with quoting Joel 2:28-32. The Holy Spirit guided his selection of the right Old Testament passage for the occasion. He did not quote from Ezekiel nor Jeremiah, who talked about a new heart and a new spirit. He quoted Joel, who prophesied about an outpouring of God's Holy Spirit that would break down barriers and energize all the people of God. After the text, Peter included explanation, argumentation, illustration, application, and persuasion.

After understanding the truths from the text, the challenge is to state the *central idea* in one good sentence. This exercise helps you determine the main thrust of the text. The lesser ideas are marshaled under the central idea. For example, in Matthew 6:5-8, the main subject is *effective prayer.* Since the text is from part of a sermon and contains instructions on prayer, the deductive approach is appropriate. The central idea could be stated as "Effective prayer involves pure motive, a private place, trust in God, and genuine communication."

The outline of the sermon puts in proper sequence the development of the central idea. The outline is for the preacher's benefit. It becomes the roadmap with signs to keep you going in the right direction. A roadmap does not bind you; it gives you freedom to travel with confidence. This outline works best for the preacher when the points are stated in complete sentences, present tense. You have explored the message to the original hearers and now you are isolating "timeless truths." The present tense indicates timeless truth and makes the sermon applicable throughout to the present hearers.

Let's note a possible outline for Matthew 6:5-8:

I. Effective praying involves pure motives.

II. Effective praying involves a private place.

III. Effective praying involves trust in God.

IV. Effective praying involves genuine communication.

Are these timeless truths? Are these immediately applicable? Does each point arise from the text? Is each point a definite part of the central idea?

These instructions from Jesus in Matthew 6:5-8 are simple and yet profound. If they are understood, accepted, and practiced, the believers' prayer lives would be revolutionized. There are other teachings on prayer in the Bible, but it is enough to deal with this text only in this sermon. The people do not need to go away impressed by the multitude of thoughts shared, but impacted and transformed by the one central idea.

Supplementary texts are sometimes appropriate. They should be researched in a similar way that you researched the primary text so you are sure of their meaning. You should be clear on why and how they are being used. They could be used to clarify a part of the primary text, illuminate the text, or add a needed ingredient to the primary text.

The expositor proclaims each point of the outline by a variety of components. These could include declaration, explanation, argumentation, illustration, and application. Each of these components answers a question. For example, *explanation* answers "What does this mean?"; *argumentation* answers "Is this true?"; *application* answers "So what?"

With our intergenerational and multicultural congregations, *illustrations* pose a great challenge. The illustrations need to accomplish a specific purpose and connect to most of the hearers. Illustrations can illuminate, emphasize, motivate, or apply. Illustrations can come from the Bible or other disciplines such as history, science, or psychology. They can be from observation, reading, or your own experiences. These should be fitting both to the content and to the congregation. Be modest with personal illustrations, and do not hurt members of your family or your congregation.

How will you *connect* the people with the body of the message the Lord has guided you to prepare? This question should be answered before you get up to speak. The congregation will usually listen for a couple of minutes to see if they need to listen further. During that time, you can help them see what you are going to be dealing with and why it is important that they hear it. People are usually motivated by "felt needs." Sometimes you have to help them feel the need. Hopefully, intellectually and emotionally, the hearers are brought into the body of the sermon. You may raise pertinent questions that you will deal with during the sermon. You may describe a scene that will connect them to the content. It may be a personal struggle you have overcome that will provide the connection needed.

What is the primary *purpose of the sermon*? The overarching purpose is transformation by the power of God. Is the specific purpose to bring individuals to salvation? Is it to equip the people of God? Is it to challenge the Christians to be involved in spiritual outreach? Is it to encourage the people? The purpose will help guide how the sermon is developed and how it is concluded.

The *conclusion* is in line with the purpose. Ask the Lord to guide you in driving home the point of the sermon and in persuading the hearers to respond positively and appropriately to the sermon. You could restate the main points. You could give an appropriate story that will serve as an intellectual and emotional climax. You may summarize what you have said and give a brief explanation. Your conclusion should round out the central idea and leave the hearers with a clear and sharp focus on the decisions demanded by the sermon.

The *title* should gain interest for the sermon even before the introduction. It should be attractive and it should give a clue about the sermon that will cause the people to want to hear what you have to say. If the title is memorable or catchy, it should help the people remember the content—if indeed you deliver what the title promises.

## Proclaiming the Message

Being confident that you have the message God wants you to share, you pray for and work toward having the best way to communicate the message.

Think about *language*. You have the opportunity to translate the ancient thought patterns and terminology of the Bible into words understood by the particular group with whom you share the message. Some of the theological terms need to be defined, described, or explained. Impressing people with difficult words is not the purpose of your sermon—communicating God's message in an understandable way is the purpose.

Choose your words carefully. Use descriptive words . . . action words . . . simple words. Preaching is primarily an *oral, aural* event—a message spoken to be heard and understood. It is not a literary composition to impress the most educated. The hearers do not have the leisure to hit "pause" and check the dictionary. The message needs to be understood as the speaker is speaking.

Choose the *method of delivery*. The proclaimer, the message content, the hearers, and the occasion contribute to your choice. Consider potential advantages and disadvantages of each method of delivery. Certain steps can help maximize the advantages and minimize the disadvantages.

In *manuscript* preaching, the minister writes the sermon completely and reads it to the congregation. If written well and read well, the sermon can be very precise and less physically and emotionally taxing than some other methods. Potential disadvantages include poor eye contact and emotional detachment. To minimize these, you need to be very familiar with the manuscript so you can make regular contact, and you need to make sure you are emotionally and spiritually involved in the reading.

In *memory* preaching, the minister writes the sermon completely, memorizes it, and then recites it to the hearers. If your memory does not fail, you have the same potential advantages as with manuscript preaching. You can also have good eye contact. Potential disadvantages are that the message could come across as one giant recitation or as more of a performance than a proclamation. You can minimize these by making sure you are fully engaged and that this is a message from your heart.

In *extemporaneous* preaching, the minister studies thoroughly and maybe has written the sermon, but the manuscript is not taken to the pulpit. The preacher may have a written outline, but the basic language used in the sermon is left until the occasion. With the depth of preparation and considering the immediate congregation, the preaching can potentially connect with the hearer with warmth and appropriateness. The potential disadvantages are that the sermon may not be as precise. For example, grammatical errors will be more likely. This method is physically and emotionally exhausting.

In *preaching without notes*, the minister seeks to internalize the message in such a way that even though the language is not memorized, the message flows from the mind and heart of the preacher. The preacher is fully engaged with the message and the people. However, the preacher risks leaving out part of the message.

Give attention to *body language*. Body language includes facial expressions, posture, gestures, and use of the voice. The preacher wants to be as natural as possible and without distracting mannerisms. Facial expressions communicate the most. The challenge is to be in touch with the message and allow the face to communicate it appropriately. For example, if you are preaching about the joy of the Lord and your face demonstrates grief and anxiety, the congregation will be confused and will likely get the message revealed by the facial expression rather than the message revealed by the words.

## Who Is Sufficient for These Things?

You pray and study and think and consecrate yourself to God. You saturate yourself with God's Word and the specific message. You try your best to relate to the hearers. You sit where they sit . . . stand where they stand . . . hear and feel their hurts, dreams, dilemmas, hopes, and hopelessness. You try to be honest with yourself and in touch with your own feelings and struggles, and this helps you understand the human situation and the desperate need that everyone has for God's message and grace. Preaching, then, can engage the anguish of the human soul, not just in pious generalities or in "holier-than-thou" demands, but with the humility of a fellow traveler in need of divine grace, direction, and provision.

If we could not depend on the Holy Spirit to be involved with us, we could not handle the challenge and stresses of preaching. If we could not depend on the Holy Spirit working through our weaknesses, or in spite of our weakness, we would have very little hope. But we *can* depend on the Holy Spirit's power to accompany the message that we share so it will have transforming power.

Paul asks that rhetorical question, "Who is sufficient for these things?" The obvious answer is "No one, without God." Note the positive statements of 2 Corinthians 2:14-17:

> But thanks be to God, who in Christ always leads us in triumphal procession, and through us spreads in every place the fragrance that comes from knowing him. For we are the aroma of Christ to God among those who are being saved and among those who are perishing; to the one a fragrance from death to death, to the other a fragrance from life to life. Who is sufficient for these things? For we are not peddlers of God's word like so many; but in Christ we speak as persons of sincerity, as persons sent from God and standing in his presence (NRSV).

Paul then says, "Not that we are competent in ourselves to claim anything for ourselves, but our competence comes from God. He has made us competent as ministers of a new covenant" (3:5-6).

We depend fully on the Holy Spirit to direct us, guide us, help us, superintend us, give us insight, and enable us. We do our best in cooperation with the activity of the Holy Spirit. We do not depend fully on our own efforts, nor do we expect the Holy Spirit to do everything. By God's grace, we move in step with the Holy Spirit and entrust the final results to Him. The praise also is given fully to God!

The preacher then can preach the Word, believing that God's intended purpose will be accomplished. The preacher can expect results—such as conviction, conversion, sanctification, baptism in the Holy Spirit, healing, deliverance, encouragement, motivation, and equipping. These and other results can be expected because *God is at work in the preaching of His Word*!

# 9

# How to Plan a Sermon Series

Marty L. Baker

It was Tuesday, but Sunday was coming. As I sat in my office, praying and preparing for the weekend message, my wife, Patty, knocked on the door. She told me that there was someone who needed to see me. Her name was Sylvia. As she sat down in my office, I could tell she was nervous. She tried desperately to appear calm and act as though everything was OK, but I could sense there was something going on deep inside. In an abrupt manner, she looked up and blurted out, "What kind of church is this?"

I responded, "We are a part of the Church of God denomination."

With great confidence she said, "Oh, *denomination* . . . I have heard of that one before."

I smiled and continued to listen to her story. Eventually she broke down and said, "I need to be honest with you. I am twenty-six years old and I have not been inside a church since I was thirteen, and then it was with a friend. My marriage is falling apart and I need help."

I sat there in disbelief, not in the fact that her marriage was falling apart, but that she had not attended church in thirteen years. How could this be? Sylvia lived within walking distance of our church, and not only our church, but there were five other denominations represented on our street. This random meeting opened my eyes to the Lord's harvest. I am ashamed to say it, but this meeting was one of the first encounters that I had personally

*Scriptures are from the *New International Version*.

had with a completely unchurched person. As a child, I was taught to come out from among the world and be separate. I did that, but I did not realize that was only a part of the equation. The full equation is that I must come out from among the world and be separate so I can go back into the world and proclaim the gospel.

Ironically, the day that Sylvia walked through our doors, our congregation carried the name Harvest Church of God. We advertised that we were a church of the harvest, but in reality we did not have a vision for the unchurched. Sylvia helped us realize there are unchurched people all around us and these individuals are headed for a Christ-less eternity. God used her to open our hearts. We have come to realize that lost people matter to God, and if they matter to God, then they ought to matter to the church.

If God's heart is for the lost, then how we communicate really matters. We must learn to speak in a way people can understand. We must speak with substance, clarity, and anointing. If we are deep without being clear, then our message will not be understood. If we are clear but do not have substance, then the words we are speaking will soon be forgotten. If we are deep and clear but do not have God's anointing, then we will not bear spiritual fruit.

How we communicate really matters. Jesus understood this, and that's why He often used parables—short stories that illustrate spiritual principles—as a method of sharing God's Word. These stories were relevant to their lives; they dealt with everyday issues like relationships, money, and spiritual fulfillment. Jesus put His audience right in the middle of the story. As they listened, they felt as though He was talking directly to them.

## An Example From Jesus' Ministry

Not only was Jesus a master storyteller, but He often tied stories together in a series of messages. We see this in Luke 15, where Jesus presents a sermon series that focused on the pain of losing something or someone. This series was designed to communicate God's heart for lost people. Jesus began the series with a message about a lost sheep. The people in His audience knew the pain of losing an animal. Many of them were shepherds or were related to someone who worked with sheep. They understood the pressure of leaving the ninety-nine to go and look for the one that was lost. He used this work metaphor to communicate God's heart for people who had lost their way.

Jesus does something that in their culture, and at that time, would seem unacceptable—He turned and looked at the women in the crowd. He was inclusive even though the culture at that time was not. In that day, a man would not even make eye contact with a woman who was not part of his family. That is why today many women in the Middle East are veiled. I am sure that people in His audience where wondering, *What is He doing?* Then they heard Jesus speak, "Suppose one of you women has ten silver coins and loses one?" (see v. 8).

At that moment, Jesus had the full attention of all of the women in the crowd. His second sermon in this series connected in a deep way with the women because every one of them received ten coins from their father. It was similar to a dowry. The women would take the ten coins and make a headdress with the coins dangling around their head. At this point, would-be husbands could see in a tangible way what this woman would bring to the table. In a cultural kind of way, their self-esteem was tied to this custom. If someone had a headdress with nine or eight coins, others might say, "Hey, you don't want her!" So, to lose a coin was awful.

Jesus turns to the women and says, "Suppose a woman has ten silver coins and loses one. Does she not light a lamp, sweep the house and search carefully until she finds it?" (v. 8). The women in the group think, *You better believe that she would!* In that day, a woman would do almost anything to get a lost coin back.

Jesus concludes His series with a message about a lost son. It is interesting how He begins with *one hundred* sheep, then *ten* coins, and now *one* son. This final message hits home because Jesus focuses on a wayward child who decided to distance himself from his father. The younger son wanted the benefits of his father's provision but did not want a relationship with him. The younger son wanted freedom; he wanted the opportunity to do what he wanted.

Jesus touched an emotional chord in each of the men as He told this story. These guys could not imagine leaving home or having one of their own sons leave home under these conditions. Jesus increases the tension in the story as He talks about the youngest son squandering his father's money and then ending up working in a socially unacceptable industry. Jesus concludes the message with the young man coming to his senses and asking his father for forgiveness. His father welcomes him home with a big party and full restoration. The people in the audience were shocked at the father's love and generosity. The point of this final message was that the heavenly Father has open arms for lost sons and daughters. God does not want to punish them, but He simply wants them to come home.

The sermon series in Luke 15 is only one example of many connected messages in the Bible. Other examples include the Ten Commandments, the letters to the churches in the Revelation, the seasons of the life of Joseph in Genesis, and so on. Connecting sermons together helps people stay engaged in the story and hopefully encourages them to come back to the next service. A series allows time for the lessons to sink in and be applied. Sometimes I expect too much from a single sermon; on the other hand, I may underestimate what can be achieved over time. Preaching is like planting seeds. We plant the Word of God in people's lives, and then that seed must be cultivated so individuals will grow in the knowledge of the Lord.

## Advantage of Sermon Series

*A series of sermons can create momentum in a church.* We discovered this at Stevens Creek Church in the fall of 2003. We introduced a series of messages based on Rick Warren's book *The Purpose Driven Life*. These messages touched a chord in our community, and people responded by coming back to hear the next message. They invited their friends to attend with them. This series produced spiritual momentum. We baptized thirty-seven new believers at the conclusion of that series. We realized that when people know what is coming, they are more likely to invite their friends to church.

*A sermon series allows messages to balance each other.* A message is out of balance when it has too much information in it. There is a tendency to go wide and not deep. I preached my first sermon when I was in high school. I still remember the points I preached in that midweek service at the Abbeville Church of God: "you need to be saved, you need to be sanctified, and you need to be filled with the Holy Ghost." The sermon lasted less than fifteen minutes. The message was wide, but it was not deep.

When I plan a series, I have the ability to cover a wide range of topics with individually deep messages. When preaching a series from one book in the Bible, or one section of a book, I can use my preparation time to really wrestle with that book. A series of five sermons in Romans allows me more time in studying that particular book and gives me a better understanding of the text. If I jump from book to book, I miss out on an opportunity to fully embrace the text.

Years ago, we took two Scripture verses—Galatians 5:22-23—and crafted a summer series on the fruit of the Spirit, called "Being the Best That You Can Be." We went deep by taking each character quality and presenting it as a stand-alone message.

This allowed people the opportunity to put into practice what they had learned in the previous week's message.

*In a sermon series, the individual messages are tied together in the theme.* This helps people stay connected to the topic and helps the preacher in the preparation process. When you know what is coming up, it helps you to focus your preparation weeks or even months in advance of the message. Pastoring a church can be stressful, and nothing is more stressful than having to stand before a congregation when you are not adequately prepared. A sermon series helps reduce stress by providing a preaching plan and a process that helps keep you centered. For example, if you are preaching a three-week series on faith, hope, and love, then you have more time to look for current stories to help illustrate the message. If you are preaching week-to-week, the pressure of illustrating the message can be daunting. As a result, you end up grabbing an illustration from someone else. It may be appropriate, but it is not personal. People want to connect with you on a personal level. A preaching plan will help you find personal stories that will help people understand how to live out their faith.

## Developing a Sermon Series

### Start With Prayer

A sermon series begins at the same place a single message would begin—with prayer. One cannot overemphasize the importance of prayer when it comes to biblical preaching. Prayer clears the junk out of our minds and opens us up to hear the voice or the promptings of the Spirit. As I consider a series of sermons, I want to know *the burden of the Lord.* I want to know what the Lord would say to the audience if He were here physically. I realize that I am a vessel. If the people are going to be spiritually moved through the message, then God must move through me during the preparation process.

Before preparing a sermon, I start with a simple prayer: "God, what do You want to say to the people?" Then I listen for His voice. On the practical side, I typically have a pen and piece of paper near and I write down any thoughts that come to my mind during this time. These thoughts may center on broad concepts like marriage or relationships. They may also focus on a book of the Bible or biblical themes like worship, discipleship, or spiritual service. The Bible is full of material, and during the preparation process, I am trying to discern the big idea for that particular day. I want to preach the whole counsel of God, but not all at one time. I understand full well that one's mind can only receive what one's seat can endure.

Once you have prayed and have the mind of the Lord, you most likely will have the mind of the people too. God wants to reach your listeners with the good news of the gospel more than you do. He wants people to grow in their faith and knowledge of the Word. God often uses the circumstances of the world to spark spiritual questions. These questions often lead people to have spiritual conversations with their friends prior to coming to hear your message. Over and over, I hear people say to me, "Marty, I felt like you were talking right to me." At other times people say, "I felt that you have been listening in on our conversations at home." God is constantly working behind the scenes. He wants people to know His Word, so He prepares them with questions or prompts conversations that will eventually lead them to Him.

### Speak the Language

As ministers we must be not only in tune with God, but with the people we are communicating with. In other words, we must engage the culture and learn to speak their language. The apostle Paul did this in Acts 17. He went to Athens and stood up in the meeting of the Areopagus. There he preached an evangelistic message. Paul engaged their pagan Greek culture by using their own statues and poets to communicate the gospel. Paul built a bridge from the culture to the Bible, and we must do the same.

A few years ago, we took this concept and made it literal. It was Easter week, and several guys in our church built a bridge that spanned the stage at our church. When I stepped up to preach that day, I said, "Here's what I want you to understand this weekend. Easter is all about a bridge, and hopefully by the end of this talk you will understand what I mean."

Continuing the message, I said: "Why do people build bridges? When you think about it, bridges can be very dangerous to construct, very expensive to build, and very costly to maintain. So, why do people go through all of the trouble to build a bridge? The obvious reason is, there is a gap between where they are and where they want to be. A bridge gets you over to the other side."

After presenting the message, I went back to the introduction to help me close: "Bridges help you get from where you are to where you need to be. You know, Easter is all about a bridge. Oh, it's not about crossing a mountain gap or a large body of water, but it's about spanning the gap between human beings and God. It's the gap between us and our Creator. So, God built a bridge. He sent Jesus Christ to this earth to bridge the gap between mankind and God. All you have to do is simply cross the bridge that He has built. The bridge is available to you regardless of what you have done. It does not matter how many good deeds you have done, or how many bad deeds you have done. God built a bridge for you to cross."

Scores of people crossed the bridge that weekend—they made Jesus Christ the leader and the Lord of their lives. We took a spiritual concept and made it literal. We spoke their language. When people understand the gospel, it is hard to resist.

Like I said earlier, the apostle Paul used cultural statues and poems to communicate the message of the gospel. We, too, must speak in a way people can understand. This is challenging because we are teaching ancient scriptures to contemporary listeners.

Never assume that people know the Bible. If you are going to begin the talk with a passage of Scripture, tell them where to look. For example, if you are preaching from the Book of Acts, say, "Turn in your Bibles to Acts, chapter 2." Then say, "The Bible is divided into two sections: the Old Testament and the New Testament. Acts is the fifth book in the New Testament—Matthew, Mark, Luke, John, and then Acts." Or, let's say you are preaching from Exodus 4. As you tell them to turn to this chapter, give a quick history lesson. You could say, "Exodus is the second book of the Bible, and it tells the story of freedom for God's people. Exodus was written by Moses, who wrote the first five books of the Bible. Sometimes people call these first five books 'The Law.' Now, turn to Exodus 4."

When you do this, you are introducing the Bible to people in your congregation. Again, do not assume that everyone knows the Bible. You are called to build a bridge from the culture to the Bible.

At Stevens Creek Church, we use creative sermon series to introduce people to faith. An example of this was our recent series called "Rock of Ages." Times have been tough and people are looking for stability. The Bible teaches us we can build our lives on a solid foundation, and when we do this, we will be able to withstand the storms that come our way. This concept of the solid foundation started to resonate with us. We developed a five-week series on the "rock stories" of the Bible. Then, to create some momentum, we chose five rock songs from each decade, beginning with the 1950s, and asked our congregation to vote on their favorite. The song that won the congregational vote was performed the next week in service.

This series generated a lot of excitement, and people invited their friends to church during this series. Many of them came to hear the music, but in the end, it was the message that changed their lives. We spoke their language. Let me pause for a moment and give some practical wisdom here. We selected the five songs that people voted on. This was an important part of the puzzle.

Music that is presented from our stage must be in keeping with the theology of our church. We will never compromise our convictions to collect a crowd, but we will learn to speak the language of the culture that all may come to faith.

On a side note: Our most popular series in the last five years has been "Gone Country." We focused on "country values," or what we understand to be "biblical values." During the "Gone Country" series, the church grew by about two hundred people.

## Flow With the Calendar

We should look at the calendar and build our series to flow along with it. Specifically, every December we will build a series that focuses on Christmas. We use a drama element that builds from week to week, leading up to our Christmas Eve services. In the earlier days, we did a Christmas play that was presented the first weekend of the month. After the play was over, our attendance went down. Several years ago, we stumbled on the concept of doing a fifteen-minute Christmas drama each Sunday of the month and crafting a message to go along with the sketch. People get interested in the storyline and come back to see what happens the next week. This has been a huge attendance builder for our congregation.

On a typical Sunday, we have around 1,800 people in church. Our auditorium seats 500, so we present four identical services each Sunday. Last Christmas, because of this drama/sermon concept, our Sunday attendance grew each week during the month of December. On Christmas weekend, we had six identical services and an attendance of nearly 3,000 people. Don't forget, our auditorium only holds 500. People are more open to the gospel message during holiday seasons like Christmas and Easter. Build sermon series that capitalize on those important times, and make sure that you speak the language of your listeners.

## Let Others Help

Ask the Lord to give you creative ideas for original sermon series, but do not be afraid to use a series from another congregation. At Stevens Creek, we created the "Rock of Ages" series, but we borrowed the "Gone Country" series from Granger Community Church in South Bend, Indiana. We created the "Re" Series—which had messages called "ReFocus," "ReGroup," "ReConnect," "ReStore"—but we borrowed the series "How to Be Rich" from Life Church in Oklahoma.

On several occasions, I have used the word *we* in talking about sermon preparation. At Stevens Creek Church, I have some preaching coaches that help me along the way. The head coach, Dave Willis, is nearly twenty years younger than me, but he is a gifted communicator and often helps me tell the story. Next, Kevin Lloyd helps me to tie life experiences to my message to help it connect with the congregation. Finally, Todd Sturgell helps create memorable moments through song and drama that allow me to speak into the hearts of the listeners.

Not only do they coach, but yes, they sometimes correct. When I step off the stage after our first service, I will ask them for feedback. They do not point out problems unless they have a potential solution. Here's an example of what they might say: "Marty, you rushed this point. Take a breath and embrace the moment before going to your next point." At other times, they may say, "You mispronounced that word; it should be pronounced this way." These guys speak into my life and my sermons because I have invited them to do so. I am a better communicator today because of my coaches.

Here's another practical idea. For years I struggled with what to preach during our Wednesday worship services. I invested so much time on the weekend that my creative energies were lacking for midweek. Chris Hodges, at Church of the Highlands in Birmingham, Alabama, gave me this idea for Wednesday nights. We currently read through the *One Year Bible* every year as a church. Pastor Hodges encouraged me to preach the *One Year Bible* passage that the congregation would be reading on that Wednesday. By doing this, I am reminding the people to stay faithful to reading their Bible, and it also encourages me to preach passages that are less familiar. In other words, it stretches me.

There needs to be a good balance in sermon series. If all you do is original, then you are probably more predictable than you think you are. If you use all borrowed sermon series, you are missing an opportunity to grow as a communicator.

Speaking of growing as a communicator, you need to listen to other great communicators. Choose preachers that have a similar heart and calling as yours. Learn their cadence, watch their delivery style, and seek to understand their anointing. The Bible says "iron sharpens iron" (Prov. 27:17). We need to grow in our ability to communicate the gospel of Jesus Christ. When our congregation was less than 150 people, Dr. David Cooper preached a revival for us. During that revival he told me, "Marty, if you want to run 1,200 people, then you must preach to 100 as if you were preaching to 1,200." I have never forgotten that. Through the years, here's what I have learned: Effective preaching is hard work. I have come to appreciate the words of King Solomon in Ecclesiastes 12:9-12:

> Not only was the Teacher wise, but also he imparted knowledge to the people. He pondered and searched out and set in order many proverbs. The Teacher searched to find just the right words, and what he wrote was upright and true. The words of the wise are like goads, their collected sayings like firmly embedded nails—given by one Shepherd. Be warned, my son, of anything in addition to them. Of making many books there is no end, and much study wearies the body.

## Creative, Engaging, and Effective

Twenty years ago, God forever changed my perspective through a lost young woman named Sylvia who wandered onto our property. Since that day, God has given our church the opportunity to reach a harvest of more than a thousand people just like her who were far from God, but have now discovered a life-changing, soul-saving relationship with Jesus. We have embraced our calling to be "fishers of men," and we have also come to realize that being a good fisherman requires using "bait" that will attract the fish!

I encourage you to see the media and messages of this culture as something that can be leveraged to point people back to the truth of Scripture and the power of God. Never water down the message, but always be willing to package it and deliver it in a way that will connect with the people we are called to reach. Let's make every aspect of our sermons and services creative, engaging, and effective. Let's live what we preach "so that in every way [we] will make the teaching about God our Savior attractive" (Titus 2:10).

Let's use every resource, technological tool, and innovation at our disposal to reach the lost and do the work God has called us to do. I'm honored to be your partner in this work, and I pray God's continued blessings for your life, your church, and your ministry!

Jesus said to His disciples, "The harvest is plentiful, but the workers are few. Ask the Lord [who is in charge] of the harvest, therefore, to send out workers into his harvest field" (Matt. 9:37-38).

# 10

# How to Preach to Diverse Cultures

### David E. Ramírez

*When this sound occurred, the crowd came together, and were bewildered, because each one of them was hearing them speak in his own language* (Acts 2:6 NIV).

One of the most glorious events in Acts 2 is the miracle of converting a *monolingual community into a multilingual community*. It is not the world's concern to speak the language of the Church, but rather it should be the concern of the Church to speak the language of the world. The gospel should be communicated in the language of the hearer. And this requires a rethinking of our work with children, young people, women, immigrants, and other groups that often do not understand us because we do not speak their "language." It was indeed for such a great task as this that the Lord gave us His Spirit: "We hear them in our own tongues speaking of the mighty deeds of God" (v. 11).

Today's church has a responsibility to reach global cities—populated by a variety of cultures, generations, ethnic groups, and nations. In the Christian faith, which has as a central claim that "the Word became flesh, and dwelt among us" (John 1:14), "preaching is compelled to be a multilingual activity, mixing

*Scriptures are from the *New American Standard Bible*.

theological terms and scriptural accounts with the artifacts of culture."[1]

The best pastoral leaders have an extraordinary capacity to understand the contexts in which they serve and to benefit from the opportunities that are presented to them in their time. In the long run, the success of a pastor (whether man or woman) is not due just to the strength of one's personality, nor to the amplitude and profundity of one's skills. Without the ability to perceive and to adapt oneself to the changing conditions of the ministerial world, personality and skills are temporal strengths. An understanding of the *Zeitgeist*,[2] or the spirit of an epoch and its implications, has played a crucial but unnoticed role in some of the greatest ministerial victories in all ages. In Christian history, we have great examples of men and women who knew how to interpret the *Zeitgeist* and to see great changes and transformations on the horizon. They were the ideal people to promote the kingdom of God in the most difficult of times. These people not only were able to do good biblical exegesis and hermeneutics, but in addition, they knew how to interpret the times and the contexts of their mission in order to be relevant and pertinent to their epoch.

## A Message of Hope

We need to become a community of worship, truth, love, and service; above all, we must become a community with a message of hope. The image we generally have of the church is that of a pastor looking out at his flock and the congregation looking back at their pastor, with their backs to the community around them. Today, we must lift up our eyes and look where Jesus looked: the city, the people, those on the outside, the immigrants and the foreigners, the lost, and those who have no hope. For this purpose, we must make radical homiletic and missional changes in order to reach those who have not been reached.

Whether it is language, music, symbols, style, or whatever they may consider beautiful, for each of the target groups we wish to reach, we need to incorporate something of their own folkloric expression. It is clear that the church service of today is not just diverse, but heterogeneous; it is a flowing together of cultures and traditions. We are in the presence of multicultural liturgies, orders of worship, in which there is an interchange between what is foreign and what is local, what is traditional and what is modern. It is important to continue stimulating these interchanges and the cultural assimilations that affirm the universality of Christian liturgy.

We could improve the quality of the liturgical services by using people in relation to their personal competencies and their spiritual gifts. Preaching is also an instrument of mission. We must find appropriate moments for where and when to invite the membership to gather around the Lord's Table. The majority of Hispanics, for instance, come from a Roman Catholic religious background where the centrality of the service is the Eucharist. The Lord's Supper has a natural attraction and is a fundamental point of contact with Hispanic spirituality.

The church of today must speak the language of the people. Contemporary preaching must adapt itself to modern times where multicultural, multilinguistic, and multigenerational communication is imperative. The language must be appropriate, used to communicate the message that will speak to the contextual needs of the different groups of people we try to reach with the wonders of God.

## Narrative Preaching

Narrative preaching can be one of the homiletic approaches that allows greater openness to communicate cross-culturally. The use of stories, images, and illustrations can help facilitate the understanding of a sermon in a heterogeneous group. Thomas G. Long said:

> The culture has shifted, and we need to take up with purpose Augustine's two other terms: *teaching* and *ethical speech*. Preaching today is going to need to learn to speak in multiple voices, some of them more direct, commanding, and urgent than narrative. The power in Christian preaching comes not only from narration but also from *declaration* ("Christ has been raised from the dead!"), *explanation* ("If for this life only we have hoped in Christ, we are of all people most to be pitied"), *invitation* ("Be steadfast, immovable, always excelling in the work of the Lord"), *confession* ("By the grace of God, I am what I am"), and even *accusation* ("O death, where is your victory?"). Every rhetorical instrument of human truth-telling needs to be pressed into the service of proclaiming the gospel, and must become obedient to that gospel.[3]

Narrative preaching must move like a good story. These stories must have a plot (suspense) moving from disequilibrium to equilibrium. This type of homiletic approach is particularly attractive to the emergent generation, which is visually oriented, and also cultures like the Hispanics that understand readily the structure of the story or narrative.

The narrative sermon is known for emphasizing biblical stories and for its descriptiveness (less explanatory and moralistic). It has a holistic character (addressing not only the intellect, but also the emotions), and uses poetic and metaphorical dimensions of language, recovering the role of the imagination in the message.

The narrative sermon is the most consistent way to communicate cross-culturally (the Bible is a book of stories, the creeds are confessions of stories, and culture is a culture of stories). The argument of the sermon is the intriguing narrative that holds the three-minute attention span of the modern hearer, and provides the strongest conduit of flow that helps the message stick (I hear, I forget; I see, I remember; I do, I understand).

The narrative sermon piques interest in all types of audiences, guides the people's imaginations, and gives life through the narrative experience (the congregation identifies with biblical characters and it gives a contemporary flavor to the biblical tradition).

The narrative sermon helps connect to cultural diversity, because people identify personally and collectively with their story in relation to the story we're telling. The objective is to intertwine the biblical, ecclesiastic, and personal story of the person who is preaching with the personal story of every listener, thus facilitating the connection with the cultural diversity represented in the audience.

## A Design for a Narrative Sermon Sensitive to Cultural Diversity

1. Learn the biblical text well.
   - Read the passage several times.
   - Find the main parts.
   - Identify each part through the use of key words.
   - Write a manuscript.
   - Memorize the manuscript.
2. Identify the characters of the narrative.
   - Shadows—characters that are barely mentioned
   - Secondary characters
   - Types—representing a class of people
   - Main characters—being fully developed
3. Study the social, political, and historical context of the biblical text.
4. Don't add details to the story.
5. Don't take away details.
6. Avoid anachronisms.
7. Keep the story in order.
8. Appeal to the listeners' feelings.
9. Use active rather than passive voice.
10. Give a contemporary flavor to the story.

11. Pay attention to personal encounters in the story.
12. Depend on the inspiration and direction of the Holy Spirit.

## Important Keys to the Sermon Oriented Toward Cultural Diversity

1. Be relevant and pertinent.
2. Search the biblical depths.
3. Don't assume anything.
4. Prefer more didactic sermons.
5. Give the sermon a conversational style.
6. Value the audience.
7. Make eye contact.
8. Move away from the pulpit to prevent its blocking of communication.
9. Get to the point.
10. Make sure the message inspires.
11. Use humor whenever possible.
12. Use stories.
13. Be authentic.
14. Prepare sermon series.
15. Preach with enthusiasm.
16. Be yourself.
17. Guard the integrity of the gospel (biblically and theologically).

# Model of a Culturally Sensitive Sermon

**Title: "Immigrants as Instruments of Mission and Vision"**

**Central Text:** "Ruth the Moabitess said to Naomi, 'Please let me go to the field and glean among the ears of grain after one in whose sight I may find favor.' And she said to her, 'Go, my daughter'" (Ruth 2:2).

The simple presentation of the protagonists of this story seems to indicate that there would be no happy ending. They are people who apparently have no future because they are in circumstances that choke life, making their very existence grueling. They are a family that doesn't even have a destiny because their present is so obscure. They can't see the horizon; they can only feel and understand their present anguish.

These are the people who were born to suffer and mourn their unsightly, never-ending tales with no signs of hope. This is a family that is the victim or survivor of hard circumstances. They have no right to dream because dreams are for other people—those with a destiny . . . those who were born with a silver spoon . . . those who enjoy power, dominion, and privileges. But those who suffer the reality of hunger, marginalization, and injustice fail to perceive any other option—only the life of migration as foreigners. This reality has become the raw experience in a globalized world where borders and cultural policies have failed to prevent or stop the movement and human displacement to and from every conceivable direction.

The last decade has been characterized by large displacements and human movements worldwide. For example, statistics from 2004 show 500,000 Ecuadorian immigrants in Spain, when in 1998 there weren't even 40,000. In immigration, this is the largest-growing group, with 60 percent of them as undocumented immigrants.[4]

The Book of Ruth says that in those days there was a famine in Bethlehem. Elimelech and his wife, Naomi, along with their two children, were experiencing need, hunger, and hopelessness in the "house of bread" (the meaning of *Bethlehem*). They must have talked frequently about their inability to meet their own basic needs. Maybe they looked for solutions, as so many Latin

Americans have, by contemplating separating themselves from their families and migrating in search of a way to break out from the permanent insecurity—the inability to resolve the most basic and elementary problems of life. Elimelech and Naomi decided to leave the land of bread to look for bread elsewhere. This history is repeated now when millions of people have to abandon their own land rich in natural resources to serve the nations that exploit the riches of their native countries.

Naomi and her family searched for a place where they could dream again, build a new life, and find hope and well-being. Apparently, the plains of Moab were the best option; we do not know why. The Moabites had always been Israel's enemies—their core values and anti-values always were an affront to Jehovah. They were polytheistic, worshiping many gods; fertility was idolized and sexual promiscuity was used to achieve divine benefits.

Of all places to migrate, this was the worst—a town that had sprung from Lot in an incestuous relationship with his daughter. It is ironic to think that, given the existential reality, the most unexpected places can become the only hope for life. In other words, God will use unexpected regions of the earth as places of temporary refuge or strategic mission platforms. Elimelech and Naomi began a long journey in search of a new destiny. Soon after arriving in the new land, Elimelech died, leaving Naomi behind, alone with her two children.

Surely she was overcome with the sadness and grief of losing a loved one in a foreign land. She became part of a very neglected group—the world of widows, the world of abandoned women. As a widowed mother, she had to face up to life in an unknown land.

Her two sons married Moabite women—questionable women not because of their character, but because they were Moabites ("they're all alike"). Somehow, probably using all her skill in relational evangelism, Naomi gained the confidence of Ruth and Orpah and brought them to know the God of Abraham, Isaac, and Jacob. Her sympathy and power of friendship managed to cross the borders of culture that separated them to bring them closer to the true light.

Tragically, Naomi's two sons died also, leaving Ruth and Orpah widows. Now there were three widows who were facing the circumstances of premature abandonment.

I admire Naomi; despite so many pains and sorrows, including her depressed state of deep mourning, she still had the strength to make a decision. She had heard there was now bread in the "city of bread," Bethlehem of Judah, and decided to return home. Naomi packed her belongings, left her home, and, together with her two foreign daughters-in-law, began the long road back. Three women who had lost their sense of direction and destination, family protection, land and inheritance now were on an open path to the unknown.

According to the Chilean philosopher Humberto Giannini, this path has unknown and disturbing depths. Just as a poet finds both opportunities and obstacles in the use of words, so the road is an expeditious means of travel, while at the same time it is "open territory in which the traveller, going his own way, may at any moment be stopped, distracted, delayed, detoured, lose himself, [and] continue forward."[5]

That was the experience of the path of Naomi. Apparently, Naomi's mood—her need to be alone, not for her own desire, but rather because she didn't have the energy even for herself, much less anyone else—made her stop in her path, and ask her two daughters-in-law to return to their home and kinsmen. Naomi is going through an emotional and spiritual crisis, and she insists that each daughter-in-law return to their respective homes—"Return to your people and to your gods" (see Ruth 1:8, 15). Her daughters-in-law weep and mourn; they do not wish to turn back. They want to be a part of something bigger; they want to be united because there is more hope in unity. They had found in Naomi a new path, a leader whom they could follow. They had found in her a sense of purpose and destiny. This foreign immigrant had shown them a different life, maybe even purpose in life—a sense of meaning.

But Naomi insists so strongly that Orpah decides to return. Something strange happens to Naomi upon sending her daughter-in-law back into the land of sin where other gods govern. Naomi loses her sense of mission to be light to the nations. Instead of thinking about mission, she's thinking about her own pain. She allows herself to be influenced by a deep sense of self-pity. She experiences a profound worry and desolation that blinds her spiritual vision and missional purpose.

In this story it is easy to confuse the identity of the immigrant. In one moment, Naomi and her family are the immigrants, and in the next, it is Ruth herself. In a sense, we all are—at one time or another—immigrants.

Something similar happens in the United States and in other countries where the foreign immigrant discovers, through the church, the blessing of the kingdom of God, but is surprised later by a church that prefers to think of its own welfare, security, and sense of self-protection. He or she realizes the church sometimes chooses to sacrifice the fruit of its mission. It is even able to develop a theology that justifies all the coldness, segmentation, and missional blindness. A church that is simply striving to survive as an organization is taking a position which radically opposes the message of Jesus.

This indolent attitude reminds me of my own experience several years ago in Southern California, where I was pastoring a Hispanic group alongside an American pastor who was responsible for his faithful "Anglos." Two years before, this pastor had invited me to start a ministry in his church to reach the Hispanic community, at that time representing 80 percent of the city. In the first year of ministry focused on the Hispanic sector, we saw a significant increase, rapidly equaling the number of Anglo parishioners. In the second year, the Hispanic group continued to grow with energy and vitality, producing apprehension and concern to the mother church that was focused on doing everything they could think of to stop experiencing sharp decline in attendance, membership, morale, and finances.

That year, the church lost its pastor and had the opportunity to consider a bilingual Hispanic pastor to direct the destiny of a church inserted in a primarily Hispanic community. To my surprise, the church at no point considered the possibility of a Hispanic pastor, but rather hired a pastor who could not work with the Hispanic community, and even asked the Hispanic pastor and his congregation to abandon its facilities. Years later, the church was almost empty and proceeded to sell the premises despite receiving several initiatives of purchase by the Hispanic sector. This story has been repeated dozens of times in states where the Hispanic influence is a strong force and where the Anglo church has lost its sense of mission.

Naomi tells her daughters-in-law she has nothing to offer them—there is no destiny with her: "I cannot give dreams or bring hope to anyone; I'm dead inside. I cannot bear fruit for you. Go home!" (see 1:11-13). But Ruth (meaning "friend") had apparently developed another level of relationship with Naomi and said: "Do not urge me to leave you or turn back from following you; for where you go, I will go, and where you lodge, I will lodge. Your people shall be my people, and your God, my God. Where you die, I will die, and there I will be buried. Thus may the Lord do to me, and worse, if anything but death parts you and me" (vv. 16-17).

Ruth was a young woman who must cope with the loss of her husband; and although foreigners were not always welcome in Israel, she decided to travel with Naomi, even knowing that her mother-in-law would not be able to guarantee a better future.

Naomi represents a church that has gone through all kinds of circumstances and has lost the horizon that God has laid out for it. When the lights go out, we find our destiny where God is present. That is where God says, "Here I am . . . I have a plan for you." By thinking of herself, Naomi failed to realize she had brought someone out of the land of evil to enter the land of the Lord. Sometimes we look for the crowds, but God looks for a person—that person He wants to use to renew the vision . . . that person who was lost but now is found. It is interesting that the solution to the unfortunate Naomi was a young foreigner. It is also interesting to note the parallels that occur between Naomi's attitude and that of the present church—a church obsessed by its own complexity and institutional problems, puzzled by its repeated losses, and which easily replaces its missionary commitment with a radical sense of survival.

Ruth represents the younger generation that does not want to go back, the emerging believers who love their church despite seeing imperfections in it. I worry that we've already lost "Orpah"—a young generation not able to resist "disease" and the rejection of its parent. We have already lost a generation. However, "Ruth" is with us not because we are irresistibly attractive, but because she loves us, is faithful to the church, cares for the church, and wants to be empowered by the church to fulfill her mission.

Ruth did not have much to offer to Naomi, and Naomi had even less to offer Ruth. But they had each other, and that made the difference in this story. What would have happened to Naomi if Ruth had also returned to Moab as Orpah had done? Perhaps she would have died of sadness. But Ruth persisted, and her persistence changed history—not only Naomi's history, but also her own. How might young Ruth have encouraged Naomi in the long trip from Moab to Israel? How might advice from Naomi open the eyes of Ruth? How many talks on the way would have chased away the ghosts of depression and discouragement?

I like to think of Ruth as the face of the young Jesus. The youth of the church are the seeds of hope, passion, and vision that, with allegiance and loyalty, wish to give their spiritual mother what she needs: a renewal of passion; love for the restoration of their mision; and, above all, the missionary work that not only brings fruit to celebrate life, but has the power to align the whole church with divine purpose.

Once in the city of bread, "Ruth the Moabitess said to Naomi, 'Please let me go to the field and glean among the ears of grain after one in whose sight I may find favor.' And she said to her, 'Go, my daughter'" (2:2). Ruth recovers a sense of destiny, and she gains a clear vision of the desired future. She tells Naomi, "I'm ready to get a job as a foreigner, and I hope the boss is handsome and single; I need to get married." She expresses a passion to succeed and fulfill the divine purpose.

Ruth is similar to the young church that, like Jesus, makes concrete plans to achieve the desired future, has an attitude of service, and is able to leave its state of comfort to achieve the purpose of God. It is not influenced by a state of weakness and conformity generated by petty attitudes and mechanical and spiritual poverty. It is regrettable to note how the established church has lost Orpah, a generation that tried to identify with the church but its institutional fervor expelled her from its system. There are important groups of people who at one time were staunch supporters of the established church, but in the road of life, that same church has rejected them, not knowing how to prioritize their interest in the church. It was deemed more important to save the institution than to invest in the new, the different, the foreign.

Destiny itself comes close to the present to drag us into God's future. Ruth meets Boaz, and Boaz invites her to the table to eat of his bread and drink from his cup. The meal is a symbol of redemption and liberation, a symbol of the power of God's intervention in personal matters. It is a symbol of value, where the foreigner becomes a vital part of God's redemptive mission.

Boaz marries Ruth, and they have a son named Obed. For ten years she had been unable to conceive, but she was now aligned to God's purpose, God's plans. Ruth presents her son to Naomi, and the women say to Naomi, "Blessed is the Lord who has not left you without a redeemer today, and may his name become famous in Israel. May he also be to you a restorer of life and a sustainer of your old age; for your daughter-in-law, who loves you and is better to you than seven sons, has given birth to him" (4:14-15).

A woman who had lost everything discovers the power of destiny. Her child would be the father of Jesse, who was the father of David, the greatest king of Israel. And from his line would come Jesus, the King of kings. In those swaddling clothes would be wrapped the fate of us all. Ruth came from a pagan foreign country, had experienced deep pain, but with great enthusiasm she met the true God. Her glorious destiny was to become the carrier of the line of the Lord Jesus. Jesus carried with Him the marks of a young foreign woman.

Carlos Van Engen states, "In the story of Ruth, the person as the agent of the mission of God combines with immigration as the means of the mission of God."6 This young foreign woman fulfills the role of realignment to the church through the work of redemption. This is where the emerging church should understand its identity and purpose. It is the emerging and immigrant church in the United States that will, in her moment, have more value for the rest of the body of Christ than "seven sons." It is the multicultural youth of North America who will finance the retirements of the aging leaders. This young, multicultural church is Ruth—she will reap the fruit of the love of God for a generation that searches for purpose and meaning in life. She will bring in the sheaves and lay them at the feet of our Lord.

# 11

# How to Preach for Pastoral Care

### Oliver McMahan

Pentecostal preaching for pastoral care is a convergence of the Holy Spirit, the preacher, and the gospel. More like a collision that transforms the preacher, this convergence comes into clear view as Jesus stepped into the synagogue in Luke 4. His coming that day became the platform for His preaching. The event reveals that the Spirit who led Him was also the Spirit who anointed Him to preach. As we probe the priorities of His preaching the gospel, we find that His preaching was profoundly pastoral.

To encounter the full impact of Christ's calling and anointing, the full texts of Luke 4:14-29 and Isaiah 61:2b-11 follow below. Both Luke and Isaiah help us define *Spirit-anointed preaching*, *the gospel*, and *preaching for pastoral care*. Let us examine these texts as we seek to discover a Pentecostal perspective of the role of preaching in caring for people in their personal, emotional, social, and family dimensions.

### Luke 4:14-29

> And Jesus returned in the power of the Spirit into Galilee: and there went out a fame of him through all the region round about. And he taught in their synagogues, being glorified of all. And he came to Nazareth, where he had been brought up: and, as his custom was, he went into the synagogue on the

*Scriptures are from the King James Version.

sabbath day, and stood up for to read. And there was delivered unto him the book of the prophet Esaias. And when he had opened the book, he found the place where it was written, The Spirit of the Lord is upon me, because he hath anointed me to preach the gospel to the poor; he hath sent me to heal the brokenhearted, to preach deliverance to the captives, and recovering of sight to the blind, to set at liberty them that are bruised, to preach the acceptable year of the Lord. And he closed the book, and he gave it again to the minister, and sat down. And the eyes of all them that were in the synagogue were fastened on him. And he began to say unto them, This day is this scripture fulfilled in your ears. And all bare him witness, and wondered at the gracious words which proceeded out of his mouth. And they said, Is not this Joseph's son? And he said unto them, Ye will surely say unto me this proverb, Physician, heal thyself: whatsoever we have heard done in Capernaum, do also here in thy country. And he said, Verily I say unto you, No prophet is accepted in his own country. But I tell you of a truth, many widows were in Israel in the days of Elias, when the heaven was shut up three years and six months, when great famine was throughout all the land; but unto none of them was Elias sent, save unto Sarepta, a city of Sidon, unto a woman that was a widow. And many lepers were in Israel in the time of Eliseus the prophet; and none of them was cleansed, saving Naaman the Syrian. And all they in the synagogue, when they heard these things, were filled with wrath, and rose up, and thrust him out of the city, and led him unto the brow of the hill whereon their city was built, that they might cast him down headlong.

## Isaiah 61:2b-11

... and the day of vengeance of our God; to comfort all that mourn; to appoint unto them that mourn in Zion, to give unto them beauty for ashes, the oil of joy for mourning, the garment of praise for the spirit of heaviness; that they might be called trees of righteousness, the planting of the Lord, that he might be glorified. And they shall build the old wastes, they shall raise up the former desolations, and they shall repair the waste cities, the desolations of many generations. And strangers shall stand and feed your flocks, and the sons of the alien shall be your plowmen and your vinedressers. But ye shall be named the Priests of the Lord: men shall call you the

Ministers of our God: ye shall eat the riches of the Gentiles, and in their glory shall ye boast yourselves. For your shame ye shall have double; and for confusion they shall rejoice in their portion: Therefore in their land they shall possess the double: everlasting joy shall be unto them. For I the Lord love judgment, I hate robbery for burnt offering; and I will direct their work in truth, and I will make an everlasting covenant with them. And their seed shall be known among the Gentiles, and their offspring among the people: all that see them shall acknowledge them, that they are the seed which the Lord hath blessed. I will greatly rejoice in the Lord, my soul shall be joyful in my God; for he hath clothed me with the garments of salvation, he hath covered me with the robe of righteousness, as a bridegroom decketh himself with ornaments, and as a bride adorneth herself with her jewels. For as the earth bringeth forth her bud, and as the garden causeth the things that are sown in it to spring forth; so the Lord God will cause righteousness and praise to spring forth before all the nations.

## Seminal Texts for Pentecostal Preaching

Isaiah 61:2b-11 and Luke 4:14-29, in which Jesus reads Isaiah 61:1-2a, are seminal texts for understanding Spirit-anointed preaching that emphasizes pastoral care. These texts have been used to emphasize classic Pentecostal, evangelistic preaching. Speaking of the term *gospel* in Luke 4:18/Isaiah 61:1, Ray H. Hughes noted:

> The word means "to announce good news, to declare, or to bring glad tidings." Jesus used this term in the opening declaration of His ministry: "The Spirit of the Lord is upon me, because he hath anointed me to preach the gospel" (Luke 4:18). . . . Some sermons serve primarily to teach . . . elaborate on a social issue . . . expound historical lessons . . . but every minister should know and remind himself that the gospel of Christ, which is "the power of God unto salvation" (Rom. 1:16), refers to Christology, to the doctrine of Christ as Savior of the world; and the minister should examine himself periodically to make sure that he builds his sermons around this basic framework.[1]

Hughes ends his quotation of Jesus' statement at the synagogue with the word *gospel*, then connects *gospel* with Paul's use of *salvation* in Romans 1:16, but does not refer to the rest of Jesus' reading of Isaiah 61. By not citing the Scripture text further, the fuller meaning of *gospel* may be missed. Salvation is critical to the gospel, but is to be understood according to Jesus and Isaiah in a full, rich, and pastoral sense. If "gospel preaching" of this text is preaching only to bring people to initial salvation or recommitments to salvation at an altar in a church service, then the full thrust of these texts—the meaning of *gospel*, and the mission of Jesus—is not communicated.

*Gospel* here is not the first item in a list of other things that follow. Rather, it is the overall topic, and what follows is a list that directs and defines preaching of the gospel. *Gospel* not only means initial believing, but also includes what happens after believing. Each point cited by Jesus and Isaiah has a traditional pastoral meaning which lends insight to the fuller meaning of the gospel. Below, the pastoral meaning of *gospel preaching* is listed in italics after the words of Jesus and Isaiah.

1. The poor: *addressing poverty of spirit and life*
2. Heal the brokenhearted: *overcoming depression, grief, stress, and so on*
3. Bring deliverance to the captives: *removal from bondages*
4. Bring recovering of sight to the blind: *able to correctly see physically and spiritually*
5. Set at liberty those who are bruised: *bringing the disabled to fuller function*
6. Preach the acceptable year of the Lord: *entering into God's provision and blessing*
7. Refer to the day of God's vengeance: *warning of God's judgment*
8. Comfort all that mourn: *ministering to those in sorrow*
9. Give beauty for ashes: *restoration out of the ashes of life*
10. Give the oil of joy for mourning: *gladness for those mourning*

11. Give the garment of praise for the spirit of heaviness: *spirit of praise instead of despair*

What is the pastoral result in the lives of those who hear anointed pastoral preaching of the gospel?

12. They may be called trees of righteousness, planted by the Lord: *being established in holiness*
13. He might be glorified: *leading lives that bring praise to God*
14. Build the old waste places: *rebuild what has been devastated*
15. Raise up former desolations: *resurrecting what has been ruined*
16. Repair the waste cities: *reclamation of cities*
17. Repair the desolations of many generations: *an intergenerational faith vision*
18. Strangers shall feed their flocks, and the sons of aliens shall work the fields: *able to rule and reign under God*
19. Named "Priests of the Lord": *represent others unto the Lord*
20. Called "Ministers of our God": *represent the Lord unto others*
21. Eat the riches of the Gentiles: *be blessed by unbelievers*
22. Boast in the glory of the Gentiles: *benefit from unbelievers*
23. Honor instead of shame: *dishonor shall be transformed into double blessing in God*
24. Everlasting joy: *never-ending joy*

What is the pastoral result in the lives of the generations of those who hear anointed pastoral preaching of the gospel?

25. Known among the nations and peoples: *their generations to follow admired even by unbelievers*
26. All that see them shall acknowledge them: *their generations to follow admired by everyone*
27. The seed which the Lord has blessed: *their generations divinely blessed*

As a result of anointed pastoral gospel preaching, Isaiah further describes the attitude and blessing of the Lord—a state that should also abide with those who receive the anointing to preach the gospel pastorally.

28. Love judgment: *love the justice of the Lord*
29. Hate robbery for burnt offering: *despise selfish or half-hearted worship and service to God*
30. Work directed by truth: *live and be rewarded by God's faithfulness*
31. An everlasting covenant: *be in covenant with the Lord*
32. Greatly rejoice in the Lord: *delight in the Lord*
33. Joyful in God: *rejoice in the Lord*
34. Garments of salvation: *God's salvation surrounding their lives*
35. The robe of righteousness, as a bridegroom wearing ornaments and as a bride wearing jewels: *be the bride of Christ, as foretold in Revelation 19*

Finally, Isaiah records the blessings that come upon anointed pastoral gospel preachers.

36. As the earth brings forth her bud: *the certainty of God's blessing*
37. As the garden causes its plants to spring forth: *the certainty of God's blessing*
38. Righteousness and praise springing forth before all the nations: *God's righteousness and praise being displayed*

It may be argued that many of the above thirty-eight items in the Scripture text are the *result* of leading people to the altar for initial salvation or recommitments to salvation. This interpretation creates an unreal dichotomy, unnecessarily separating the gospel from all of the benefits of the gospel. This categorizes "gospel preaching" as *evangelistic*, and "preaching the benefits of the gospel" as *pastoral care*. The unnatural dichotomy is that *gospel* is one kind of preaching that leads individuals to initial or recommitted salvation, and *pastoral* is another kind of preaching that is for those who are already Christians. However, Isaiah 61 and the words of Jesus show pastoral benefits of the gospel are part of what it means to *preach the gospel*. All of the thirty-eight items listed are connected and complementary, defining what *gospel* means.

While these themes apply to someone who needs to accept Christ as Savior, they also apply to those who know Christ. These thirty-eight items are a working definition for pastors and the care they provide. "Salvation" is not just initial believing. Anointed preaching requires preaching for pastoral care. Preaching is not only to win the lost, but it is profoundly to shepherd or pastor those who have begun the life of faith.

John Chrysostom (d. AD 407), one of the early church fathers, was known for his preaching. The power of Chrysostom's sermons "was attributable in part to his zeal for souls and love for his congregation."[2] Chrysostom valued the connection with his congregation. He said, "My congregation is my only glory, and every one of you means much more to me than anyone of the city outside."[3] While Chrysostom also preached to those in the "city outside," he was affirming the value of those in the congregation.

## Why Pastoral-Care Preaching Is Important

Pastoral care as part of the gospel is important because of the anointing of the Spirit. The Spirit anoints the entire process, preaching for initial or recommitted believing as well as the pastoral care that follows. Pentecostals should not invest more in evangelism than they do in pastoral care because of a misperception that *evangelistic preaching* is "gospel preaching," and therefore more Spirit-anointed—leaving *pastoral-care preaching* misperceived as not being as much about the gospel and somehow less anointed. The gospel is pastoral. The Spirit anoints to preach the full gospel.

The office of the *evangelist* (Eph. 4:11) is distinct from the office of *pastor/teacher*. The emphasis of Luke 4 and Isaiah 61 is that both preach the gospel. The gospel includes initial believing and recommitments to salvation at the altar—much of the focus of an evangelist. It also includes the pastoral work involved at and after the altar—much of the work of a pastor/teacher. The offices of evangelist and pastor/teacher complement each other and fulfill what it means to preach the gospel with the anointing.

Pastoral-care preaching as gospel preaching is important because of the presence of Jesus through the proclamation of the Word. Dietrich Bonhoeffer said in his lecture, "The Proclaimed Word":

> In the proclaimed word, according to the promise, Christ enters into His congregation which in its liturgy adores Him, calls unto Him, and awaits Him. In the proclaimed word, Christ is alive as the Word of the Father. In the proclaimed word, He receives the congregation unto Himself . . . only through this Word are we able to recognize God.[4]

As the preacher proclaims the Word, Christ enters and ministers the gospel pastorally to the congregation. The congregation responds to Christ as they respond to the proclaimed Word. The preacher, if truly anointed, will enhance rather than hinder the work of Christ by not drawing attention to himself/herself. As Bonhoeffer noted in the same lecture:

> The preacher does not therefore accomplish the application of the word; he is not the one who shapes it and forms it to suit the congregation. With the introduction of the biblical word, the text begins moving among the congregation. Likewise the word arises out of the Bible, takes shape as the sermon, and enters into the congregation in order to bear it up. This self-movement of the word to the congregation should not be hindered by the preacher, but rather he should acknowledge it.[5]

Pastoral counselor and preacher Howard Stone emphasized that the proclaimed Word is from God himself, not the person proclaiming the Word. Stone writes, "To recast the Word in modern times, or heroically attempt to proclaim it in spite of all odds, may be to forget that the power of the Word is from God and not from what we do to parse it, adorn it, disguise it, or even improve it."[6]

Pastoral-care preaching of the gospel is important because of its connection and application to the human condition. The anointing for such preaching requires the preacher to be profoundly involved in the humanity of her/his congregation or audience. Bonhoeffer noted, "Preaching has the dual objectives of establishing the Christian congregation and building it up."[7] He further noted:

> The proclaimed word is the Christ bearing human nature. . . . This proclamation of the Christ does not regard its primary responsibility to be giving advice, arousing emotions, or stimulating the will—it will do these things, too—but its intention is to sustain us.[8]

Through the preached Word, Christ himself pastors the congregation, transforming their present humanity to a new humanity—one fashioned unto Himself by Christ. Pastoral-care preaching of the gospel does not allow constructs, ideas, themes, or illustrations to do anything short of addressing the human condition of those hearing the Word. This requires the pastor to be profoundly aware of the human condition. The desire of Christ the Word, even the proclaimed Word, is to transform individuals into a new human condition.

Jesus sees the hearers of a sermon in all of the dimensions of their human condition; the preacher must also. Preaching of the gospel must be in pastoral care and must be directed at the human condition.

## Christ Ministering to Personal Needs Through the Preached Word

Pastoral care reaches into personal lives, and so must gospel preaching. The personal level of life involves character, struggle, conflict, secret keeping, and isolation, among many other conditions. Steven J. Land notes, "Praise and proclamation, the presence of Jesus and the Spirit, and the affections in Christ and the power of the Spirit are all fused in a call to Christian character and vocation."[9] Pastor John R. Claypool said:

> Authentic preaching catches all the faculties of the human beings involved in the process—their minds and bodies and emotions as well as their tongues and ears. Thus it can be rightly called an event, something that happens so wholistically that it leaves the kind of impact on one that accompanies participation in any sort of decisive happening.... The first thing preachers must do is to acquaint themselves with the general contour of the human saga, to learn what is involved functionally in floating down the stream of personhood—infancy, childhood, adolescence, young adulthood, middle adulthood, and finally, old age.[10]

Preaching is itself, in part, a personal experience for the preacher and the hearers. Daniel E. Albrecht notes that Pentecostal "congregants, particularly during the rite of worship and praise, receive encouragement to make their worship very personal and deep.... As a result, the Pentecostal/Charismatic ritual creates a cultural domain for deeply felt expressions of human experiences." Albrecht was reporting on a study of three Pentecostal congregations. He concluded that "the pastoral message . . . expresses the worldview of the congregation; that is, the message helps, in all three of the churches, to give voice to a common definition of the 'things that matter most.' The preaching enables a 're-experiencing of a biblical text.' The pastoral message identifies it as a prophetic announcement, directed and empowered by the Holy Spirit."[11]

Preaching that addresses personal needs proclaims texts of Scripture as they reach into the personal lives of individuals found in the Bible. Examples of this include:

- The inner dynamics of Saul as he slowly compromised his character

- The anguish of Samuel as he dealt with a slowly corrupted Saul
- The inner ups and downs of David's soul as reflected in the Psalms
- The agony of Jesus in Gethsemane as He prayed about the cross and the betrayal of Judas
- The personal consequences of not obeying the wisdom of Proverbs
- The contemporary personal struggle to not have the same allegiance to money as one has to God
- The personal agony felt by the father of the prodigal, and every parent who watches for a wayward child

In this process of pastoral-care preaching, the preacher is more than a mouthpiece simply repeating what the Lord says. The preacher expresses his or her humanity through the sermon, complementing the ministry of Christ. In preaching, God chooses human instruments to convey the gospel to humanity and thereby transform them into a new humanity. As a result, Christ the incarnate Word is proclaimed through the "incarnated" preacher. The preacher is "incarnated" in that just as Christ came and dwelt in our humanity, an effective pastoral-care preacher of the gospel also dwells in his or her humanity and the humanity of the hearers.

## Christ Ministering to Emotional Needs Through the Preached Word

Emotions can conquer the soul left to itself. Whether anger or peace, despair or delight, lust or love, individuals hearing a sermon are in the midst of emotional transition, if not emotional chaos. The sermon, when proclaiming the gospel as pastoral care, can be the means of Christ ministering to a suffering saint. Leslie Allen wrote, "In general, church services can be uncomfortable and unsatisfying for the one who grieves, for these services may reflect an aversion to sorrow that takes no account of the somber realities of life."[12]

The preacher, much as Christ does, must enter into the emotional suffering of the hearer and minister. Allen noted:

> In the Book of Psalms, the worship leader speaks for a while as an individual, expressing a conviction the rest of the congregation is not yet ready to aspire to and so guiding them toward a stronger faith (Pss. 44:4-6; 74:12-17; 123:1). This worship leader, mentor, and reporter presents himself as a wounded healer, another role model for the congregation alongside Zion . . . a therapeutic ritual to deal with grief.[13]

Indeed, the sermon, as with the task of pastoring, is much of what was actually intended by the ancient definition of *psychology*. The practical theologian Friedrich Schleiermacher (1768-1834) argued that "guidance of souls" was the heart of the meaning of ancient *psychology*. He wrote:

> All of the specific tasks related to church leadership are part of what the Greeks called *psychologia*. I refer to the Greek expression directly because it is at home there. The term is easily translated as "guidance of souls"… the concept of guidance of souls has always been present in the church.[14]

In applying "guidance of souls" to preaching, he emphasized that the sermon is the work of the Spirit:

> A sermon should be the work of the Spirit, and in this sense we need only be concerned that the Spirit is truly alive. But there is something between the preacher and those in whom faith is to be awakened—the purity of the medium. Were we to ask if one becomes an outstanding preacher by possessing great talent and by following the rules of oratory, we would have to conclude the answer is no. Unless this talent [oratory] is accompanied by a living conviction about what is said to a Christian congregation, and an interest in it, no amount of talent can produce an outstanding preacher.[15]

The role of the "living conviction" of the preacher, as a work of the Spirit, calls the preacher of the gospel to take on the grief, sorrow, and emotion of the hearers. This process fulfills the ministry of Christ as described in Isaiah 53:4-5:

> Surely he hath borne our griefs, and carried our sorrows: yet we did esteem him stricken, smitten of God, and afflicted. But he was wounded for our transgressions, he was bruised for our iniquities: the chastisement of our peace was upon him; and with his stripes we are healed.

This "carrying of sorrows" is a message to be communicated, not just of Christ, but by the preacher who proclaims Christ and participates in the ministry of Christ. The preacher bears grief and sorrows through the Word. Isaiah 53 itself asks about the participant and proclaimer of this process in verse 8, "Who shall declare his generation?" Pastoral-care preaching of the gospel, when addressing the emotional condition of the hearers, is part of this declaration.

Much of what happens to emotions through a gospel sermon is healing. Randy Maddox, a Wesleyan theologian, noted that when John Wesley "turned detailed attention to the actual process of our spiritual healing, it was the 'Person' of the Holy Spirit that came into focus. Thus, the image of Holy Spirit as Physician complements that of Christ as Physician. Wesley stressed so frequently that his preachers should preach Christ 'in all his offices.' "[16] Pentecostals, as those who emphasize the work of the Spirit, should especially view Spirit-anointed gospel preaching as proclamation of the Word that heals the emotions through the Holy Spirit.

Returning to the list from Luke 4 and Isaiah 61 noted earlier, much of the direction and definition of Spirit-anointed *gospel preaching* addresses healing of the emotions (numbering from previous list is retained):

2. Heal the brokenhearted: *overcoming depression, grief, stress, and so on*
8. Comfort all that mourn: *ministering to those in sorrow*
9. Give beauty for ashes: *restoration out of the ashes of life*
10. Give the oil of joy for mourning: *gladness for those mourning*

11. Give the garment of praise for the spirit of heaviness: *spirit of praise instead of despair*
23. Honor instead of shame: *dishonor shall be transformed into double blessing in God*
24. Everlasting joy: *never-ending joy*

## Christ Ministering to Social Needs Through the Preached Word

Pastoral-care preaching that is Spirit-anointed addresses the social context of the congregation. Ray Anderson wrote:

> The ministry of proclamation, for example, will be radically determined by how we understand the Incarnation. If the Word of God stands only as an abstract or existential possibility separated from the historical context in which it originally came, then the ministry of proclamation will have no dogmatic basis for its content. Scripture will necessarily be appropriated to the latest style of cultural interpretation and hermeneutics—the act of making meaningful will itself be the primary source for revelation. Proclamation will seek to actualize all possibilities in hope of producing an event of revelation.[17]

The proclaimed Word is given in a historical context originally and addresses a specific context today, which is a social one involving real people. Further, as the proclaimed Word takes into account the context, originally and today, the revelation of God occurs in the lives of the hearers. However, if the preacher does not address the social needs of the congregation, revelation through the Word does not occur for them.

Individuals and events a preacher refers to and reads about in Scripture had real social contexts. Abraham was radically called from the social context of Ur to the social context of a foreign land, affecting much of his journey of faith. Elimelech and his wife, Naomi, along with their sons and daughters-in-law (one of whom was Ruth), experienced many difficulties: economic hardship, displacement, death, multiculturalism, living in a foreign country, widowhood, living in a country dominated by a pagan religion, the family unit being made up of two non-blood relatives, a mother-in-law and daughter-in-law, and a family returning to its homeland. The Book of Revelation is set in an end-time social context dominated by the harlotry of money and commerce (chs. 17-18). All of these settings relate to social contexts today.

Spirit-anointed pastoral-care preaching engages the whole person and social encounters as found in Scripture. They are similar, if not duplicate, of the social journeys of congregations, individuals, and families throughout time and in every place. The gospel is social in that the Word describes lives of people in their social context. Therefore, the proclamation of the Word must be revealed in the social context of its hearers. The Word is contextual, not in that it changes from one social context to another; rather, that the same Word can be applied to different social contexts and transform lives and those very social contexts into the image of Christ and His kingdom.

The earlier listing of Luke 4 and Isaiah 61 addresses several social applications, albeit transformations by the gospel as it is preached with the anointing (numbering from previous lists is retained):

1. The poor: *addressing poverty of spirit and life*
3. Bring deliverance to the captives: *removal from bondages*
14. Build the old waste places: *rebuild what has been devastated*
15. Raise up former desolations: *resurrecting what has been ruined*
16. Repair the waste cities: *reclamation of cities*
18. Strangers shall feed their flocks, and the sons of aliens shall work the fields: *able to rule and reign with God*
21. Eat the riches of the Gentiles: *be blessed by unbelievers*
22. Boast in the glory of the Gentiles: *benefit from unbelievers*
38. Righteousness and praise springing forth before all the nations: *God's righteousness* and praise being displayed

Not only are social contexts addressed in the above list, but the gospel advocates for change and transformation. The Spirit-anointed preacher of the gospel becomes an advocate to transform the poor, captives, wasted places, desolate places, wasted cities, strangers, aliens, places of unbelief, and nations. The preacher as advocate means being more than an observer, commentator, or condemner; rather, he is a reformer, a rebuilder, even an instrument of "resurrection" as Christ is revealed and ministers through the preached Word.

Inherently, by being social, the preached gospel always addresses relationships. All of the law of the Old Testament is fulfilled by a relational commandment—to love one another (Gal. 5:14). The law of Christ is fulfilled in a relational commandment to bear one another's burdens (6:2). The gospel is known through the relationships believers have for one another (John 13:34-35). If the gospel is to be known, the preacher of the gospel must address social relationships within and without the community of faith. The community of faith becomes a model for society in general through the preached Word. Dorothy Bass notes that preaching is so connected to the community of believers that preaching itself is a practice of the community and not just the individual preacher:

> Because preaching is such a shared practice, it demands a response. . . . The preacher is a witness who searches the Scriptures on behalf of the community and then returns to the community to speak what he or she has found. . . . Preaching is the practice of the whole church and not of the preacher alone.[18]

**Christ Ministering to Families Through the Preached Word**

Social dimensions of Spirit-anointed gospel preaching lead to relationships, especially those in the family. The gospel itself is directed to families, not just individuals. Gospel preaching has been westernized and thereby secularized by its overemphasis on the individual's encounter with God, with not enough attention to the family and the intergenerational nature of faith. Initial believing is not just the beginning of one person's journey of faith. It is true that one person cannot confess and believe unto salvation for another person, even a member of one's family. However, faith is the result of what happened in previous generations and is concerned with what happens to future generations. Our families have been fragmented in part because preaching has only been directed to individuals.

Spirit-anointed preachers must proclaim that God saw Adam and Eve as a family.

- It was a brotherly dispute that led to Cain's killing Abel.
- Noah and his whole house was spared from the Flood.
- Rahab and her whole house were delivered from destruction at Jericho.
- The allotments of land to the tribes of Israel were actually "inheritances" to be passed from one generation to the next.
- Joshua determined that he and his house would serve the Lord.
- The generations of Jesus were the first thing said about Him in Matthew's Gospel.
- On the cross, Jesus instructed the disciples to care for His mother.
- The New Testament calls us "the family of God."
- God is supremely addressed as our Father.
- The ultimate, eternal description of the Church is as the bride of Christ.
- The New Jerusalem is described as a city "prepared as a bride adorned for her husband" (Rev. 21:2).

The gospel of Jesus, as cited earlier in Luke 4 and Isaiah 61, is one to the generations—families, not just individuals. The gospel for the generations/families means the following:

17. Repair the desolations of many generations: *an inter-generational faith vision*

25. Known among the nations and peoples: *their generations to follow admired even by unbelievers*
26. All that see them shall acknowledge them: *their generations to follow admired by everyone*
27. The seed which the Lord has blessed: *their generations divinely blessed*
35. The robe of righteousness, as a bridegroom wearing ornaments and as a bride wearing jewels: *be the bride of Christ, as foretold in Revelation 19*

## The Scandal of Spirit-Anointed Preaching

The hearers of Jesus' proclamation in Luke 4 were scandalized by what they heard. The preacher who follows the same pattern of Spirit-anointed preaching can expect no less today. The pastor's preaching is no less anointed than the evangelist's. Yet, any preacher who preaches the gospel in all of its personal, emotional, social, and family dimensions as described by Jesus and Isaiah will experience resistance.

Jesus gave two examples of what this kind of preaching looked like in verses 25-27—Elias (Elijah) proclaiming to the widow of Sarepta (Zarephath), and Eliseus (Elisha) proclaiming to Naaman. All of the thirty-eight items in Luke 4:18-19 and Isaiah 61:2b-11 listed earlier apply to these two examples. This was the full gospel preached. It addressed the personal, emotional, social, and family dimensions of the widow and Naaman: a poor widow who was destitute, neglected, and alone; and an alien outcast who came to be healed.

Jesus' preaching that day, and the examples He used, endangered His life (Luke 4:28-29). How dangerous is it to preach the gospel for pastoral care? The real danger is to have a vision as a preacher that goes no further than one trip to the altar to pray the sinner's prayer. Certainly, that trip is the necessary beginning. However, the gospel that God holds all preachers accountable for sees the one trip to the altar as only a place of beginning. The gospel message is incomplete with that one trip, and so is preaching that does not include pastoral care.

# 12

# How to Give an Effective Altar Call

**Janice Claypoole**

*Now then, we are ambassadors for Christ, as though God were pleading through us: we implore you on Christ's behalf, be reconciled to God* (2 Cor. 5:20).

## A Meeting Place

The altar is the meeting place between God and His people. The Hebrew word for "altar" is *mizbeyakh*, meaning "a place of sacrifice" (place of slaying). It is a place where we die to our will and submit to the will of God. The altar is a place where the Divine connects with the mortal. It is a place of dialogue between God and humanity that results in a response from God!

When the first wave of tens of thousands of Hebrews returned from seventy years of exile, the first part of God's house they rebuilt was the altar. Once built, "they offered burnt offerings on it to the Lord" (Ezra 3:3). They wanted God to be with them, so they "built the altar . . . to offer burnt offerings . . . as it is written in the Law of Moses" (v. 2).

In many churches today, we need to "rebuild" the altar. The altar service has traditionally been a focal part of the Pentecostal worship service, but in too many churches the altar no longer receives the attention it deserves.

*Scriptures are from the *New King James Version* unless otherwise indicated.

Let's change this! Because our people need to meet with God, and because the altar is one place where this should be happening, let's do all we can to emphasize ministry at the altar.

## A Place of Remembrance

When the Lord appeared to Abraham at Shechem, promising him, "To your descendants I will give this land," Abraham responded by building an altar to the Lord (Gen. 12:7).

When the angel of the Lord appeared to Gideon, the farmer feared for his life. But the Lord spoke peace to him. "So Gideon built an altar there to the Lord, and called it The-Lord-Is-Peace" (Judg. 6:24).

For both Abraham and Gideon, the altars they built were altars of remembrance. These were monuments of rock they could point to and say, "The Lord spoke to me here."

Believers need such monuments! How wonderful for an individual to be able to point to an altar and say, "I remember when God answered my prayer as I cried out to Him there."

## A Place of Cleansing

When Isaiah saw a vision of the Lord in the Temple, he cried, "Woe is me, for I am undone! because I am a man of unclean lips . . . for my eyes have seen the King, the Lord of hosts" (Isa. 6:5). Then an angel removed a hot coal from the altar and touched Isaiah's lips with it. The angel said, "Your iniquity is taken away, and your sin purged" (v. 7).

There is nothing more siginificant than seeing an unsaved individual have his guilt taken away as he or she kneels before God at an altar. We must regularly give people the chance to receive Christ at a church altar.

## A Place of Healing

Jesus said that if you approach an altar and then remember that someone has something against you, you must "first [go and] be reconciled to your brother, and then come and offer your gift" (Matt. 5:23-24).

In our day, countless people have lives filled with fractured family relationships. They need to know Jesus is concerned not only about their relationship with Him, but also about their relationships with others. In fact, the two go hand in hand. He wants to help them to forgive and to receive the forgiveness of others.

## A Place of Intercession

When God sent a terrible plague upon Israel because of their rebellion against Him, "David built there an altar to the Lord, and offered burnt offerings and peace offerings. So . . . the plague was withdrawn from Israel" (2 Sam. 24:25).

Today, God will use church members in the ministry of intercession if we will so train them at our church altars. He will use them to help bring about revival.

## A Place of Thanksgiving and Praise

When Noah's feet touched dry land after endless months in the ark, the first thing he did was build "an altar to the Lord" and "offered burnt offerings on the altar" (Gen. 8:20).

When Solomon dedicated the Temple to the Lord, the glory of the Lord filled the place. When the people "saw how the fire came down, and the glory of the Lord on the temple, they bowed their faces to the ground on the pavement, and worshiped and praised the Lord, saying: 'For He is good, for His mercy endures forever' " (2 Chron. 7:3).

As we minister the Word of God, we should teach people how to worship the Lord at the altar and provide opportunities for them to do so. Let us linger with them until the glory of the Lord fills the place! Let us also show them the necessity of developing a lifestyle of praise and thanksgiving.

## A Place of Personal Consecration

The apostle Paul understood the altar as a place of personal consecration. He wrote, "I beseech you therefore, brethren, by the mercies of God, that you present your bodies a living sacrifice, holy, acceptable to God, which is your reasonable service" (Rom. 12:1).

Abraham exhibited his complete consecration to God when he placed his dear son Isaac on an altar in obedience to God's command (Gen. 22:1-14).

## A Place to Learn

Maybe you have never thought of the altar as a teaching tool, but it should be. As the Israelites prepared to enter the Promised Land, Moses told them, "When you have crossed the Jordan into the land the Lord your God is giving you, set up some large stones. . . . Build there an altar to the Lord your God, an altar of stones. . . . And you shall write very clearly all the words of this law on these stones you have set up" (Deut. 27:2, 5, 8 NIV).

Every time the Israelites would see this stone "billboard," it would remind them of who had brought them into Canaan and how they were to live. This altar would be an ongoing teaching visual.

In our day, the altar should still be a place of instruction. This does not mean we have to engrave the laws of God on our altars (though that might not be a bad idea). It does mean when an individual seriously responds to an altar call, we have a "teachable moment" in our hands. We can give brief instructions from the Word of God and then pray with the seeker. The altar should be a place where God's people learn lessons they will never forget.

## An Ambassador for Christ

The minister acts as an ambassador for Christ, pleading for people to be reconciled to God. Paul wrote: "God was in Christ reconciling the world to Himself, not imputing their trespasses to them; and has committed to us the word of reconciliation. Now then, we are ambassadors for Christ, as though God were pleading through us: we implore you on Christ's behalf, be reconciled to God" (2 Cor. 5:19-20). Therefore, the minister preaches with purpose to bring the seeker to a place of response.

## Four Types of Altar Calls

Let us examine four types of altar calls: (1) the altar call for salvation, (2) the altar call for deliverance, (3) the altar call for healing, and (4) the altar call for the baptism in the Holy Spirit.

The altar call is simply giving individuals the opportunity to respond to the message of the finished work of Calvary. The benefits of the Cross are inexhaustible, of course, with the first benefit being salvation of the soul. Through the finished work of Calvary, there is deliverance of the captive and healing for the body, mind, soul, and spirit.

### Altar Call for Salvation

The message of salvation must be prepared with the lost in mind. Salvation is to be preached with passion and spiritual application. When preaching to the lost, it is not the minister's job to convict of sin but to present the gospel of Jesus Christ and His finished work on the cross. The preacher needs to explain that Jesus was and is the propitiation for all sin. The sin debt is paid in full.

Preach God's faithfulness to forgive sins. If we ask for forgiveness, "He is faithful and just to forgive us our sins and to cleanse us from all unrighteousness" (1 John 1:9). We need to explain how repentance brings a new beginning to the seeker's life. We need to preach that whenever God forgives, He makes all things new and their sins are cast "as far as the east is from the west" (Ps. 103:12), never to be remembered against them anymore.

When giving an altar call, we should have the worship team sing songs that speak of God's love, such as "Amazing Love." We should sing songs that tell of the price Jesus paid to redeem us back to God. We should sing songs of God's awesome mercy and forgiveness, and speak gently to reach the very heart and soul of the lost.

Altar workers must be prepared for the altar call. When people begin to respond, trained workers should be ready to meet those who decide to give their hearts to God. The altar worker should allow the seeker to pray for a few minutes privately, and then the altar worker should pray for wisdom and discernment as how to approach and pray with them.

Many times the seeker is self-conscious, heartbroken, and even afraid. The altar worker should also be aware that many times the seeker doesn't even know how to pray. If this is the case, the altar worker should lead them in the prayer of salvation.

When the seeker is finished praying, the worker should give the seeker a response card to fill out their name, address, and phone number should they want a pastoral call. The seeker should also be given material to help with their new life. One good resource is *Getting Started*, by Bill George.

### Altar Call for Deliverance

When extending an invitation for deliverance, the minister should speak clearly that Jesus came to set the captive free. Explain that Jesus faced Satan in the wilderness of temptation and was "in all points tempted as we are" (Heb. 4:15), but He came out on the other side in the power of the Spirit (Luke 4:1-14). He gained total victory over sin, not by using His divine powers, but as a man dependent on the Holy Spirit. The Scripture-based message of deliverance is that Jesus overcame the works of the devil and all that are bound can go free. "For this purpose the Son of God was manifested, that He might destroy the works of the devil" (1 John 3:8).

When giving the altar call, assure the seeker that God is a deliverer and that He will break the chains of bondage from anyone who will ask. You should also have trained altar workers experienced in deliverance ministry. They should know how to pray the Word and lead the person by faith to the delivering power of God.

### Altar Call for Healing

The minister should preach on the healing power of God based on biblical promises such as 1 Peter 2:24: "Who Himself bore our sins in His own body on the tree, that we, having died to sins, might live for righteousness—by whose stripes you were healed." The minister should preach that healing is in the Atonement, being paid for at the whipping post, and by Christ's stripes we are healed.

Testimonies from people who have been healed would be appropriate at this time to build the faith of the seeker. When the seeker responds to the healing message, trained altar workers should be available. They should know how to pray the prayer of agreement and stand on Mark 16:17-18: "These signs will follow those who believe . . . they will lay hands on the sick, and they will recover."

### Altar Call for Baptism in the Holy Spirit

The minister should preach on receiving the power of God for service (Acts 1:8). The seekers should be told to seek for power to witness and that the Holy Spirit is a gift for all believers. When the altar call is given, the altar workers should be ready to pray with the seekers to receive this powerful gift by faith. They should allow the Holy Spirit to speak. Altar workers should be trained to answer all questions the seekers may have.

In my experience, I have leaned on the Holy Spirit to direct me in each altar call. He will always quicken my spirit and help me say and do what is effective for that moment, for our ministry is " 'not by might nor by power, but by My Spirit,' says the Lord of hosts" (Zech. 4:6).

## Five Guidelines

Far too many people have had a negative experience at a church altar caused by the unwise action of a preacher or altar worker. Yes, we can hinder people instead of helping them when giving an altar call and meeting people at the altar. Here are five guidelines we should follow.

1. *Prepare your heart and theirs.* As a minister, it is your job to pray, fast, and get in tune with God's heart in preparation for delivering the gospel and helping people to receive it. Before you preach a message, you must measure yourself by it. If you are not living up to it, your people will know . . . sooner or later.

2. *Be specific.* At the conclusion of your message, make your altar call specific. For instance:
- If you have never asked Jesus to forgive you of your sins . . .
- If you want to pray for an unsaved friend or family member . . .
- If you need to be healed . . .
- If you have not been filled with the Holy Spirit . . .

3. *Know why they responded.* No matter how specific your altar call, people might respond for different reasons. Rather than assuming why someone came forward, it is always best to ask. Then you and the altar workers can pray most helpfully with them.

4. *Motivate with the Word.* As you encourage people to come forward, do not try to manipulate their emotions. Instead, motivate them with the Word of God, which is the source of genuine faith. For instance:
- The Bible says, "The blood of Jesus Christ His Son cleanses us from all sin" (1 John 1:7). Will you come forward and ask Him to forgive you today?
- The Bible says God wants all people to "come to repentance" (2 Peter 3:9). Will you come forward and pray for someone you know who needs to accept Jesus Christ?
- The Bible says "God shall supply all your need" (Phil. 4:19). If you have a need only God can meet, will you ask Him to help you?

5. *Rely on the Holy Spirit.* I have seen people saved, filled with the Spirit, called into ministry, healed, and delivered at church altars. In every case, it is the Holy Spirit ministering

through the Word of God that has done the work. If we want to see people's lives changed at the altar, we must rely fully on God.

# 13

# How to Preach With Integrity

**Thomas Lindberg**

*Now a bishop must be above reproach. . . . He must manage his own household well. . . . He must not be a recent convert, or he may be puffed up with conceit and fall into the condemnation of the devil; moreover he must be well thought of by outsiders, or he may fall into reproach and the snare of the devil* (1 Tim. 3:2, 4, 6-7 RSV).

We have all said: "Come on, let's be honest." That common expression can apply to many areas of life, but it supremely applies to preaching. When a man or woman stands before a crowd to preach, they are proclaiming God's eternal truth (see John 17:17). Since they hold the truth-filled Word of God in their hands, it is incumbent that what comes out of their mouths is truthful.

Paul instructs Timothy that a preacher must be "above reproach" (1 Tim. 3:2). He tells Titus that God's messengers need to be "blameless" (Titus 1:6). Let me say big, bold, and clear: There are high ethical standards that we must maintain when we prepare and present a sermon from God's Word.

Preachers who desire to sharpen their skills and effectiveness must ask at least three questions about preaching. First, "What shall I preach?" That will determine the content of the message.

---

*Scriptures are from the *New International Version* (2011) unless otherwise indicated.

Next, "Why do I preach?" That will determine the conviction of the message. Finally, "How should I preach?" That will determine the character of the messenger. Each question deserves a clear answer.

In this chapter, I focus on the final question: "How should I preach?"

## Integrity in Sermon Development

The word *integrity* comes from the world of mathematics, where its root is *integer*. By definition, an *integer* is a whole number in contrast to a fraction. *Integrity* implies that an individual is a whole person marked by complete honesty and is not a fractional individual who sometimes is honest while at other times is not. That has enormous implications for those who preach.

Paul urged the younger pastor: "Do your best to present yourself to God as one approved, a worker who does not need to be ashamed and who correctly handles the word of truth" (2 Tim. 2:15). Greeks who refined gold used the word "approved" (*dokimos*). Once they removed all the impurities from the ore, they formed the gold into bars and stamped *dokimos*, that is, "impurity-free." This is how preachers must view their task as they prepare to proclaim God's Word. They must maintain high ethical standards as they assemble the material they preach.

This means we must be accurate in handling the Scripture text from which we will preach. It is wrong at best, and dishonest at worst, to twist a biblical passage to make it say what we desire it to say. The Bible is not a soft lump of clay God places in our hands so we can mold it to whatever shape and form we choose. Instead, it is a proven, settled rock of revealed truth that we need to humbly and diligently explore for its truth to emerge. The Holy Spirit not only inspired the biblical passage from which we will preach, but He also illuminates the messenger so he or she can be an accurate, anointed spokesman for God.

The Bible sits above us to guide us how to live and what to preach. We do not sit above the Scripture to determine our own standards or concoct our own messages. The prophet Micaiah said, "As surely as the Lord lives, I can tell him [King Ahab] only what the Lord tells me" (1 Kings 22:14).

Consider the words of John Calvin a month before he died as he was saying goodbye to some preachers: "I have not corrupted one single passage of Scripture, nor twisted it as far as I know. I have always studied to be simple and clear." A good rule of thumb is this: Do not develop a sermon from a text if only one Bible version translates it the way you desire. Let multiple translations confirm your conclusion.

Another mark of integrity is that we will not preach another person's sermon. To do so is unethical. I received a letter from a pastor who told me he listened to my sermons on the radio and then preached them a few weeks later in his church. Real preaching occurs when preachers communicate to their congregations what the Holy Spirit has revealed to them through their personal study and interaction with the Scripture. One benefit of preparing a sermon is that the Holy Spirit not only helps you develop the message, but He also develops you.

Deuteronomy 5 has an instructive verse on the dynamics of true preaching. The people said to Moses, "Go near and listen to all that the Lord our God says. Then tell us whatever the Lord our God tells you. We will listen and obey" (v. 27). Good preaching must include a personal witness. Yes, you will read other commentators, writers, and speakers during preparation; but integrity demands and the Spirit desires that the finalized message must have your thoughts, prayers, and fingerprints all over it. You and I can milk many cows as we prepare to preach, but we must churn our own butter.

If all we desire to accomplish through our preaching is to inspire our people or explain a biblical text, then why not just play a DVD from some gifted, nationally known preacher instead of wasting our time preparing? That is insufficient, because God's people want a personal witness to the power of God. If God is not speaking to you, how can He speak through you? People desire to see the Word of God become flesh in their pastor, and then, in turn, have their pastor guide them so they can successfully navigate life and please God. That is integrity in the development of a life-changing message.

## Integrity in Sermon Delivery

In preaching, "the Word becomes flesh" (see John 1:14). To use the words of Phillips Brooks, "Preaching is God's truth communicated through human personality." Who the preacher is—his words, her emotions, his body language, his passion, her dress—cannot be hidden. Who we are as preachers will ooze out in our sermon. Therefore, it is imperative we demonstrate integrity in both our sermon development and delivery.

Some point to Philippians 1:15-18 as proof God can use any kind of sermon delivery—good or bad, ethical or unethical. While it is true that our sovereign God can use any preached sermon, it would be foolish to lower standards to conclude integrity in delivery does not count. Paul is not urging anyone to follow the example of the jealous preachers in Philippians 1. That passage is the exception, and you do not build principles off the exceptions, but off the norms.

Think of Paul's inspired autobiography as he reveals how he preached. In 1 Thessalonians 1:5-6 he wrote: "Our gospel came to you not simply with words but also with power, with the Holy Spirit and deep conviction. You know how we lived among you for your sake. You became imitators of us and of the Lord, for you welcomed the message in the midst of severe suffering with the joy given by the Holy Spirit." Then, in 2 Corinthians 2, he added, "Unlike so many, we do not peddle the word of God for profit. On the contrary, in Christ we speak before God with sincerity, as those sent from God" (v. 17).

What must we learn from Paul? We must preach to please God. It is possible to undo in your delivery what the Holy Spirit accomplishes in you during your preparation. Excessive pointing to self is not pleasing to God during delivery. Humility must mark the preacher. Humility is not putting yourself down, but it is lifting up the Lord Jesus Christ. Our God-given duty is to "preach Christ" and not self (see 2 Cor. 4:5). Name-dropping will also hurt your delivery. As you drop names, you are saying, "I know important people. That makes me important as well."

Any breach of pastoral confidence will also harm your delivery (and also the person whose confidence you broke). During the week, you rub shoulders and interact with many people. You will hear of successes and failures, victories and sins. To publicly share the successes and victories of others without permission is foolish and possibly damaging. To publicly reveal the sins and failures of others is wrong.

In the 2 Corinthians 2 passage quoted above, Paul tells us we are not to be like people who "peddle the word of God." The verb "peddle" comes from the Greek noun *kapelos*—a con artist, a street hawker, or a huckster who would say and do anything to manipulate people. Too many today peddle a message that does not have a biblical foundation. These peddlers do not bring glory to God, nor do they see real-life transformation in people. Their main goal is self-enrichment. We must guard our integrity as we deliver God's message.

Preachers need both righteousness and godliness. We best understand the difference when we view *righteousness* as affecting our outward conduct, while *godliness* affects our inner attitude. For the most part, God's people want to trust the person who stands before them to preach. But integrity for the preacher is a precious commodity. With it, people will follow you; without it, they will not. To quote Billy Graham, "If you lose your money, you've lost little. If you lose your health, you've lost something important. But if you lose your integrity, you've lost everything."

Preachers must lean hard on God as they deliver the message (see 1 Cor. 2:1-5). It is not our clever gimmicks that convert and challenge others. It is the Spirit of God using the Word of God. If we persuade someone to trust Christ merely by our clever argument or delivery skills, it is probable that someone with a more clever argument or greater speaking skills may deceive them. It is the Spirit, not human skill, who brings transformational life change into the human heart (see Zech. 4:6). To deny this truth is to deny our present existence as people who are led and empowered by the Holy Spirit (see 2 Cor. 5:7). That's real integrity in the delivery of a life-changing message.

## Integrity in Sermon Decision

The purpose of a sermon is not primarily to inform the mind; its purpose is to transform the heart. That means a preacher should call for some kind of a decision at the end of every sermon. Just as a good insurance salesman would not think of showing a client a new insurance product without asking if he would like to buy it, so you need to preach each sermon for decision.

The first recorded sermon in Acts is Peter's clear explanation and powerful challenge in chapter 2. Here is how the apostle finished: "With many other words he warned them; and he pleaded with them, 'Save yourselves from this corrupt generation' " (v. 40). Peter was clear in his call for a decision.

The integrity of the messenger matters greatly as we call people to decision. Phillips Brooks defined *preaching* as "God's truth through human personality." It is possible to run clean water through a dirty pipe, but I would not want to drink it. As you compare that analogy to preaching, the implications are clear and convicting. There are many jobs in our world today where the character of the person doing the work really does not matter that much. Preaching is not one of those jobs.

The integrity of preaching is front and center in 1 Corinthians 2: "I came to you in weakness with great fear and trembling. My message and my preaching were not with wise and persuasive words, but with a demonstration of the Spirit's power, so that your faith might not rest on human wisdom, but on God's power" (vv. 3-5). Paul refused to use calculated theatrics or human techniques to manipulate a response. Do not get people to respond to your emotional appeal instead of to the true knowledge of God and the conviction of the Holy Spirit.

Martin Luther faced this problem. As the Protestant Reformation began to spread, some of Luther's followers resorted to manipulation, force, and less-than-honest methods of preaching to sway people. Luther would have none of it. In spring 1522, Luther marched to his pulpit and said, "I will preach, teach, and write, but I will constrain no man by force. I could play little games, but what would happen? A fool's play. I leave it to God's Word." That is integrity in asking people to follow Christ.

Charles Spurgeon—a beloved pastor, a great preacher, and a powerful evangelist—preached for a decision and saw tens of thousands come to Christ. He focused on the integrity of the preacher when calling people to decision, and wrote words that are difficult to improve: "The power that is in the gospel does not lie in the eloquence of the preacher, otherwise men would be the converters of souls; nor does it lie in the preacher's learning, otherwise it would consist in the wisdom of men. We might preach until our tongues rotted, till we would exhaust our lungs and die, but never a soul would be converted unless the Holy Spirit be with the Word of God to give it the power to convert the soul."

Good preaching will always contain three essential components: (1) what is said (*logos*), (2) how it is said (*pathos*), and (3) who says it (*ethos*). First Thessalonians 1:5 rolls all three components into thirty words: "Our gospel [*logos*] came to you not simply with words but also with power, with the Holy Spirit and deep conviction [*pathos*]. You know how we lived among you for your sake [*ethos*]."

Some years ago, I looked up the word *preach* in *Merriam-Webster's Dictionary*. The second entry said, "to exhort in a tiresome manner." Nothing could be further from the truth. Your preaching must be faithful to the Bible, birthed out of a life of integrity, and dynamic to the listener so that lives will be transformed.

The words of Robert Murray M'Cheyne are as true today as when he wrote them in 1840: "Remember you are God's sword—His instrument. In great measure, according to the purity and perfections of the instrument, will be your success. It is not great talents God blesses so much as great likeness to Jesus. A holy minister is an awful [awe-inspiring] weapon in the hand of God." Amen.

May you rise to God's calling and be the best preacher you can be!

*Reprinted from *Enrichment Journal* (winter 2013 issue). Used with permission.

## CONCLUSION

# The Uniqueness of Spirit-Filled Preaching

**Lee Roy Martin**

*While Peter was still speaking these words, the Holy Spirit fell upon all those who heard the word* (Acts 10:44).

One Sunday after church, I ate lunch with a group of college students from various denominations and backgrounds, one of whom was my nephew who had gathered this group together. One young man asked another if he would be going to hear a certain preacher, and he replied, "No, I'm not going. I don't really like his style of preaching. He's too loud, he yells a lot, and I just don't care for it."

His answer intrigued me, so I inquired, "What kind of preaching do you like?" He explained that he enjoys listening to preachers who are more refined, and whose sermons are more like a lecture.

Lively discussion ensued, with several other students throwing in their comments. A young man from the Bahamas talked about the great preaching in his home country, and he shared how the people would take delight in sermons that lasted as

*Scriptures are from the *New King James Version*.

much as one or two hours. He said that in the Bahamas they love exciting, passionate preaching.

When I left that little luncheon, I felt that something had been missing in the conversation, but I could not put my finger on it. We had talked about preaching only in terms of externals—like the length of the sermon and the style of delivery—but surely there is more to preaching than those things. As I drove home, I wondered if we Pentecostals can claim anything distinctive in our preaching. As I began to think and pray about this concern, the Lord showed me there is an element of Pentecostal preaching that we had omitted from our discussion that afternoon. At that moment, I felt something deep in my soul, a fire burning in my heart that exemplifies Pentecostal preaching. The Spirit of the Lord came down in my car and the Spirit spoke to me these words from the Book of Acts: "While Peter was still speaking these words, the Holy Spirit fell upon all those who heard the word" (10:44).

I cried out, "Hallelujah!" Yes, that is the answer. The distinctiveness of Pentecostal preaching is not a matter of style or manner of delivery. It is not a matter of sermon type, sermon length, or the number of scriptures that are quoted. The distinctiveness of Pentecostal preaching is something deeper and more fundamental than externals. It is a hunger and thirst for the life-giving, transforming presence of God. The goal of Pentecostal preaching is that God himself will come down in the midst of the congregation.

Daniel Albrecht argues that for Pentecostals, the entire worship service "is aimed toward an *encounter*" with God.[1] In his article "Community and Worship," Jerome Boone argues that the "single most important goal of any Pentecostal worship service is a personal encounter with the Spirit of God."[2] The Holy Spirit will break into the service, and something wonderful, something powerful, something apostolic will happen when the Word of God is preached. The goal of Spirit-filled preaching is that every hearer will be filled with the same Spirit that fills the preacher.

When I preached my first sermon in 1973, the ministry of Pentecostal preaching was unambiguous and well-defined. Young preachers faced few variables and entertained few options. The most difficult choice in those days was whether we would emulate Ray H. Hughes, T. L. Lowery, or Paul L. Walker in our style of preaching. There were no YouTube videos to introduce the sermon, and no PowerPoint slides with which to highlight important points. Churches had no spotlights, sound effects, or projectors. Preachers rarely considered the possibility of using creative arts or objects as illustrations. Today, however, the choices are endless, and the opportunities for creative preaching are limited only by our imagination. Preaching is more challenging today than ever before, and we must take advantage of these new methods and approaches if we are to remain effective in the twenty-first century. It is hoped that this book will encourage every preacher to declare the gospel with creative enthusiasm, innovation, and integrity.

However, while we open our hearts and minds to new and exciting methods of preaching, we must also take care to remember the essence and heart of Pentecostal preaching. Our creative methods must not become a substitute for the power of the Holy Spirit; rather, we must pray and believe that the Holy Spirit will use every method for His glory. In this chapter, I suggest the goal of Pentecostal preaching is that the hearers will be transformed by the Holy Spirit. No matter what preaching method we decide to use, we must keep the ultimate goal before our eyes, in our minds, and in our prayers.

As we examine Peter's sermon from Acts 10, we will discover four important characteristics of Pentecostal preaching.

## 1. Pentecostal Preaching Is Unique in Its Origin.

In order for Pentecostal preaching to reach its goal of divine encounter and transformation, *the sermon must be birthed in prayer.* According to Acts 10, Peter went up to the housetop about noon. Why did he go there? Was he reading his Bible commentaries? Was he surfing the Internet for illustrations? Was he checking the news for current events? No, Peter went up to the housetop to pray. The preparation for a Pentecostal sermon is the prayer closet.

While study is necessary in building an effective sermon, and knowledge of the times is essential for making the sermon relevant, neither study nor insight can give birth to a Pentecostal sermon. In order to bring ourselves to the spiritual place where the Spirit will move when we preach, we must get "on top of the house" and begin with prayer. The message must be born out of a heart of prayer, because when we are in prayer, we receive more than an exposition—we receive a burden from the Lord. When we are in prayer, we get more than just a sermon—we receive a message from God. In Pentecostal preaching, the sermon is a prophetic message, a "burden" (Mal. 1:1). Pentecostal preaching is passionate—it is the release of the Word, which is like a "fire shut up in [our] bones" (Jer. 20:9). This burden cannot be obtained in any way except by prayer, fasting, devotion, and times of testing.

But that is not my main point. Let me move on.

## 2. Pentecostal Preaching Is Unique in Its Content.

While Peter was on the housetop praying, God gave him some content for his sermon. It came in the form of a vision, as God reached down and spoke to him.

> [Peter] saw heaven opened and an object like a great sheet bound at the four corners, descending to him and let down to the earth. In it were all kinds of four-footed animals of the earth, wild beasts, creeping things, and birds of the air. And a voice came to him, "Rise, Peter; kill and eat." But Peter said, "Not so, Lord! For I have never eaten anything common or unclean." And a voice spoke to him again the second time, "What God has cleansed you must not call common." This was done three times. And the object was taken up into heaven again (Acts 10:11-16).

Peter knew God had given him a vision, but he did not quite understand it. He had to meditate on it, and his reflections resulted in a prophetic message from God.

While he was pondering the vision, three men arrived from the house of Cornelius, a Roman centurion. They requested that Peter come and speak to a group of people gathered at Cornelius' house. Later, as Peter preached the gospel to this assembly of prayerful Gentiles, he referred to his vision, explaining God had revealed to him that he should call no one, not even a Gentile, "common or unclean" (v. 28). A Pentecostal sermon begins where the prayers of the people (e.g., Cornelius), the vision of the preacher, and the purposes of God intersect.

Later on in his sermon, Peter expounded on what has become a classic verse for Pentecostals: "How God anointed Jesus of Nazareth with the Holy Spirit and with power, who went about doing good and healing all who were oppressed by the devil, for God was with Him" (v. 38). Peter's preaching is an example of sound Pentecostal theology. We believe that just as Jesus was anointed with the Holy Spirit, so also we are anointed to preach deliverance to this world.

The heart of Pentecostal theology is the "fivefold gospel." We believe Jesus is our Savior, sanctifier, Spirit-baptizer, healer, and soon-coming King, and we must preach accordingly. The preaching of this gospel of Christ is the "power of God to salvation" (Rom. 1:16). People are hurting. They are facing unprecedented challenges. They need salvation, deliverance, and healing. They need the power of the Holy Spirit for daily living, and they need hope for the future. It is the preaching of this full gospel that has transformed the Pentecostal Movement from its small and humble beginnings into the greatest revival in Christian history. Pentecostals now number over 500 million worldwide.[3] The phenomenal growth of Pentecostalism is a direct result of sound Pentecostal preaching and the life-changing effects of that preaching. Light-weight, shallow sermons that only gloss over the hurts and put bandages on wounds are not sufficient to change lives. A Pentecostal sermon will have Pentecostal content.

I encourage you to read good sermons . . . as many as you can. We should read the sermons of great preachers of the past and the present, because "iron sharpens iron" (Prov. 27:17), and we should adapt and use their material. However, we should not attempt to preach someone else's message unless the Holy Spirit makes it our own. We must seek God for a Spirit-filled burden from the Lord.

Peter received a revelation from God, and that revealed word became his sermon at Cornelius' house. A Pentecostal sermon should emerge from moments of revelation, and those revelations will exalt Christ and minister to people. At times we are tempted to preach other kinds of revelation—revelation of our intellect, our cleverness, and our ability to manipulate people. Revelations of our own gifts and abilities are not helpful and will not save the lost. We need more than a neatly arranged argument and exposition; we need a message from God. Pentecostal preaching will speak of dreams, visions, testimonies, the acts of God, and the power of God. If we preach Pentecostal sermons, people will hear from our hearts. They will feel our burden and our passion, because if we are excited about serving God, it will be evident in our preaching.

Still, that is not my main point. Let me move on.

## 3. Pentecostal Preaching Is Unique in Its Delivery.

To say that Pentecostal preaching is unique in its delivery does not mean every preacher must utilize the same type of delivery. Every preacher must develop a style that matches his or her gifts, callings, and ministry context. Furthermore, if we are to be effective, we should modify our preaching style so it is appropriate for the audience. We would not speak to children in the same manner we speak to teenagers. We must learn how to communicate within our particular cultural context. Peter's sermon in Acts 10 is a good example of contextual preaching. His sermon in Cornelius' house was very different from his sermon on the Day of Pentecost, because he was addressing a different audience. Sometimes our context will include both church members and the unchurched (who know nothing about the Bible). Sometimes our context will include people not only from our own culture but also from other cultures and ethnic groups. On any given day, our preaching context may include women and men, the young and the old, the educated and the illiterate, the poor and the rich. It is a colossal challenge to preach effectively to the diverse audience that faces us today.

Although Pentecostal preachers will adopt an infinite variety of individual styles, we can identify traits common to all Pentecostal preaching. Following are four examples of the power of the Holy Spirit.

*First*, Pentecostal preaching is unique in its delivery because *the sermon is delivered with passion*. The burden of the Lord will produce a passion. When we have a burden from the Lord, we will appeal to more than just the minds of our hearers—we will appeal to their hearts. We will appeal to the whole person. The entire person will be addressed in a Pentecostal sermon.

*Second*, Pentecostal preaching is unique in its delivery because *the sermon will be preached with divine unction*. Too often we preach what is a weak excuse for a sermon, and then we justify ourselves by saying, "I did my best." However, our best is not what God wants. God never asked that we do our best. He asked us to pray, fast, and immerse ourselves in the Word of God until we are filled with the Holy Spirit and filled with the message He wants us to proclaim. God does not ask for our ability, neither does He ask for our skillfulness. He wants to divinely enable us. He doesn't want our best; He wants *more* than our best. He wants us to believe for the impossible. Paul admitted we are not "sufficient of ourselves . . . but our sufficiency is from God" (2 Cor. 3:5). He also declared, "When I am weak, then I am strong" (12:10).

*Third*, Pentecostal preaching is unique in its delivery because *it includes the gifts of the Holy Spirit*. A Pentecostal preacher will preach with charismatic gifts, with words of wisdom and knowledge, with healings and miracles, and with discernment. After Jesus rose from the dead and commissioned His followers to spread the gospel, "they went out and preached everywhere, the Lord working with them and confirming the word through the accompanying signs" (Mark 16:20).

Those signs, wonders, and spiritual gifts are evident throughout the Book of Acts. In chapter 2, the multitude was astounded when they witnessed the sign of tongues. They marveled and said, "We hear them speaking in our own tongues the wonderful works of God" (v. 11). In chapters 3 and 4, the healing of the lame man opened the door for Peter to preach to the crowd and see about five thousand people converted. Even the Jewish authorities admitted reluctantly, "For, indeed, that a notable miracle has been done through them is evident to all who dwell in Jerusalem, and we cannot deny it" (4:16). In chapter 5, "a multitude gathered from the surrounding cities to Jerusalem, bringing sick people and those who were tormented by unclean spirits, and they were all healed" (v. 16). Afterward, the apostles were thrown into prison, but that night an angel appeared miraculously and delivered them (v. 19). Many other examples from Acts could be included here, but let us conclude this point with the following summary statement: "Through the hands of the apostles many signs and wonders were done among the people" (v. 12).

When the crowds saw the boldness of Peter and the disciples, they realized "they had been with Jesus" (4:13). The people also said of the apostles, "These who have turned the world upside down have come here too" (17:6). Like the apostles, a Pentecostal preacher may turn things upside down. Pentecostal preaching is not always smooth. Sometimes it can be a little harsh and rough around the edges, but it is the kind of preaching that will touch people's hearts.

## The Uniqueness of Spirit-Filled Preaching

*Fourth*, Pentecostal preaching is unique in its delivery because *Pentecostal preaching is worship.* Both the preacher and the congregation worship God during the act of preaching. Jeremiah testified, "Your word was to me the joy and rejoicing of my heart" (Jer. 15:16); and David exclaimed, "I rejoice at Your word as one who finds great treasure" (Ps. 119:162). Pentecostal preaching is not a lecture in which the speaker is speaking only to the listeners and the listeners are hearing only the speaker. In a Pentecostal sermon, the preacher sees not only the people, but God also. The act of preaching is an act of worship, in which the preacher stands in God's holy presence, with one eye on God and the other eye on the congregation, with one foot on earth and the other foot in heaven, with one hand reaching up to God and the other hand stretched out to the people. The people also worship—they look both to the preacher and to God as they yield to the Holy Spirit.[4] God Almighty participates in the service as well. He is looking down and saying, "Amen, amen."

This is Pentecostal preaching. The delivery is a worship experience.

But that is not my main point yet. Let me move on.

### 4. Pentecostal Preaching Is Unique in Its Expectation.

What do we expect in good preaching? Most of us would be quite satisfied with a sermon that achieves the three *I*'s (informative, interesting, inspirational); the three *C*'s (captivating, charming, creative); the three *R*'s (rich, real, relevant); the three *P*'s (purposeful, productive, profound); the three *M*'s (meaningful, masterful, motivational); or the three *E*'s (engaging, entertaining, eloquent). Let us read about Peter's sermon from the "Contemporary Religion Version":

> While Peter preached, the people sat quietly, occasionally laughing at his subtle humor and jotting down his clever points and closely following the printed outline. When he finished, they all affirmed that they would put into practice the relevant principles that had been expounded so insightfully in his excellent

sermon. They shook his hand and said they had enjoyed his sermon immensely. Peter, after he had collected his offering, congratulated himself on a job well done. And he and a group of friends went out to Olive Garden for lunch. They discussed how far the church had progressed in these last few years. By Monday morning, they had forgotten the excellent sermon, except for the jokes, and once again they fought the same demons they had wrestled with the week before. The clever sermon had not delivered them from depression, anger, fear, hatred, lust, self-righteousness, pride, envy, or strife.

This contemporary tongue-in-cheek version of Peter's preaching is not meant to offend those of us who take notes or those who eat at Olive Garden. It is meant to critique our low expectations. Too often we are satisfied with sermons that are entertaining, informative, and inspirational, but Peter's sermon accomplished much more. His sermon produced changed lives.

Let us review what the Bible tells us about Peter's preaching:

> Peter opened his mouth and said . . . "The word which God sent to the children of Israel, preaching peace through Jesus Christ . . . how God anointed Jesus of Nazareth with the Holy Spirit and with power, who went about doing good and healing all who were oppressed by the devil, for God was with Him. . . . To Him all the prophets witness that, through His name, whoever believes in Him will receive remission of sins." While Peter was still speaking these words, the Holy Spirit fell upon all those who heard the word. And . . . they heard them speak with tongues and magnify God (Acts 10:34-46).

While Peter preached the Word, the Holy Spirit fell on all those who heard it! The Holy Spirit interrupted Peter's sermon!

To say the Holy Spirit *fell* on them suggests suddenness and forcefulness. Without warning and without planning, the Holy Spirit descended on the people in a miraculous way. We cannot schedule the moving of the Holy Spirit, but we can pray for it and expect it. We sometimes hear the Holy Spirit is a "gentleman,"

## The Uniqueness of Spirit-Filled Preaching

but here the Spirit moved in with violence. Sometimes the Holy Spirit will knock us down (see Rev. 1:17); lift us up on our feet (Ezek. 3:12); fall upon us (11:5); or unsettle us and shake us and we will feel an overpowering presence of God—an awesome display of the power of God (Isa. 6).

Suddenly, without warning, the Holy Spirit falls and we forget who we are, because we see who God is. We forget where we are, because God has said, "Come up here" (Rev. 4:1). We forget what time it is, because we are "in the Spirit on the Lord's Day" (1:10). We forget about the circumstances all around us, because we begin to see that "the whole earth is full of the glory of God" (see Isa. 6:3).

The longing for God's presence is described repeatedly in early Pentecostal literature. For example, Alice Flower wrote, "All I seemed to sense was a deep craving for the overflowing of His love in my heart. At that moment it seemed I wanted Jesus more than anything in all the world."[5] Reflecting on her passion for God, Zelma E. Argue said, "My whole heart seemed to be just one big vacuum craving and crying for God."[6] Chris Green insists "Pentecostal spirituality is nothing if not a *personal* engagement" with God.[7] Rebecca Jaichandran and B. D. Madhav agree: "The Pentecostal is not satisfied until he or she has had an experience with God. . . . A person is not satisfied by hearing about someone else's experience with God; they must experience God themselves."[8]

*Yes, this is my main point.* This is what makes Pentecostal preaching unique. This is what makes it distinct from all other preaching. We should feel free to utilize any style of delivery; we should feel the liberty to preach with a manuscript or without one; and we should use the latest technology. However, our effectiveness will be judged by the transformation of our listeners, and that transformation can be accomplished only by the presence and power of the Holy Spirit.

As Pentecostals, we expect God will transform our lives during the worship service in a way that cannot be achieved through sermons that address only the mind. God is alive and active, and He will come down in our midst. We read in Hebrews 4:12 that God's Word is "living and powerful, and sharper than any two-edged sword." God spoke through Isaiah the prophet, "So shall My word be that goes forth from My mouth; it shall not return to Me void, but it shall accomplish what I please, and it shall prosper in the thing for which I sent it" (55:11). From Azusa Street until now, Pentecostals everywhere have insisted on the present reality of God's presence to save, sanctify, fill with the Holy Spirit, heal, and reign as coming King.[9]

We have a right to expect God will move when we preach His Word. Pentecostal theologian Keith Warrington writes: "Two pertinent words when referring to Pentecostal spirituality are 'expectancy' and 'encounter.' Pentecostals expect to encounter God. It undergirds much of their worship and theology and may even be identified as another way of defining worship."[10] The Gospel of Mark tells us the disciples "went out and preached everywhere, the Lord working with them and confirming the word through the accompanying signs" (16:20). Paul explained we are ministers "not of the letter but of the Spirit" (2 Cor. 3:6). Of his own preaching, he testified, "My speech and my preaching were not with persuasive words of human wisdom, but in demonstration of the Spirit and of power, that your faith should not be in the wisdom of men but in the power of God" (1 Cor. 2:4-5). Reading these powerful Scripture texts makes me want more than a relevant sermon—I want a *revolution*; more than motivation—I want *transformation*. I want the empowering, the prophetic. I expect to see people saved, delivered, and healed—that God will be in the midst of His people.

Admittedly, I have preached some dead sermons where nothing amazing happened, but I still expect God to honor His Word. No matter how badly we fail, we should pick ourselves up and go back to our prayer closet. If we will be faithful to pray and fast, God will surprise us with revival. We cannot even begin to imagine what God can do; He can change lives right in the midst of our preaching.

*Pentecostal preaching is unique in its expectations.* We encounter God, and this encounter will often include the manifestation of spiritual gifts, and the worshipers will experience "the Spirit as transformational power."[11] Thus, we expect that when we preach and prophesy, the "dead bones" will rise up again (Ezek. 37). We believe that when we preach, we will hear "a sound from heaven," like "a rushing mighty wind," filling all the house (Acts 2). When we begin to preach the burden of the Lord, the demons will run for cover, and the devil himself will look for the nearest exit. Every time we step into the pulpit to preach, we should expect to see the Lord "high and lifted up" (Isa. 6:1). We should expect that the heavens will open and we will see visions of God (Ezek. 1:1). When we say to the sick, "Rise, take up your bed" (John 5:8), we should expect them to rise up. When we say to the afflicted, "Silver and gold I do not have, but what I do have I give you" (Acts 3:6), we should expect them to receive from God.

The Lord has anointed us to "preach the gospel to the poor." He has sent us "to heal the brokenhearted, to preach deliverance to the captives, recovering of sight to the blind, to proclaim the acceptable year of the Lord" (see Luke 4:18). We should trust that every time we get in the pulpit, the Lord God of Israel is walking in the midst of the camp to deliver us (Deut. 23:14). Every time we preach, we should anticipate the fulfillment of God's promise: "'Not by might nor by power, but by My Spirit,' says the Lord of hosts" (Zech. 4:6). Every time we preach, we should believe that "where the Spirit of the Lord is, there is liberty" (2 Cor. 3:17). We should anticipate that the hungry will be filled, and the thirsty will be satisfied. We should be confident in God's Word that says, "I will pour water on him who is thirsty, and floods on the dry ground; I will pour My Spirit on your descendants, and My blessing on your offspring" (Isa. 44:3).

When we preach, we must expect sick people to be healed, burdens to be lifted, sins to be forgiven, and lives to be changed. Let us expect God to be glorified. Let us expect weeping, mourning, shouting, praising, and people pouring out their souls before God. Let us expect the fire to come down and consume us as we have laid ourselves on the altar of sacrifice (1 Kings 18:38). We must expect it to happen. We must expect the walls of doubt and fear to crumble (Josh. 6:20). We must expect our sons and our daughters to prophesy (Acts 2:17). We must expect to see God's power and glory in the sanctuary (Ps. 63:2).[12] This is what we should expect in Pentecostal preaching.

## CONCLUSION

In a recent article, Pastor Johnathan Alvarado elaborates on the distinctive characteristics of Pentecostal worship: "Spirit-filled worship is marked and characterized by a vivid awareness of the presence of God and the activity of the Holy Spirit within the lives of the saints and within the context of the worship experience."[13] If we cease to anticipate the outpouring of God's Spirit, we will shake ourselves one day like Samson, and we will not even realize the Lord has departed from us.

We must not model ourselves after anything less than the example of the apostles. We must not become entertainers who continually try to outdo one another. Hungry souls need more than entertainment. They do not need to be pacified, or to be petted and placated. They do not need an experience of gratification and ecstasy. What they need is intimacy with God and with one another in the house of God. What they need is a refreshing from the presence of the Lord (Acts 3:19). With God's help, our preaching can open the door to that refreshing. Let it be said of us, "While they were preaching, the Holy Spirit fell on all those who heard the Word!"

# Endnotes

## Chapter 2

1. Sigmund Freud, quoted in *First Things*, by Wilfred M. McClay, *www.firsthings.com*, May 2011 (accessed Feb. 28, 2013).

## Chapter 3

1. Dale Carnegie, quoted by *www.brainyquote.com*.

## Chapter 4

1. Sam Shoemaker, quoted on *www.bible.org* from Em Griffin, *The Mindchangers*.
2. Richard Stoll Armstrong, *The Pastor as Evangelist* (Philadelphia, Pa.: Westminster, 1984).
3. Gardner C. Taylor, *How Shall They Preach?* (Elgin, Ill.: Progressive Baptist Publishing House, 1977).

## Chapter 5

1. Tim Hill, *Beyond the Mist: A Quest for Authentic Revival* (Cleveland, Tenn.: Tim Hill Ministries, 2010) 155-157.
2. *The Ecclesiastical History of Eusebius Pamphilus* (Grand Rapids: Baker, 1988) 49.
3. *www.worldchallenge.org*
4. Ibid.
5. *www.lifeandlibertyministries.com*
6. *www.goodpassage.com*

## Chapter 6

1. David T. Olson, *The American Church in Crisis* (Grand Rapids: Zondervan, 2008) 137.
2. David Kinnaman, *unChristian* (Grand Rapids: Baker, 2007) 79.
3. Kinnaman.
4. Kinnaman, 47.
5. Material adapted from Ron Bennett, *Intentional Disciplemaking* (Colorado Springs: NAV Press, 2001) 14-20

## Chapter 7

1. Paul Wilson, *Setting Words on Fire: Putting God at the Center of the Sermon* (Nashville: Abington, 2008) 165.

2. Raewynne Whiteley, *Steeped in the Holy* (Lanhan, Md.: Crowley, 2008) 113.
3. Whiteley, 114.
4. Keith Whitt and French Arrington, *Issues in Contemporary Pentecostalism* (Cleveland, Tenn.: Pathway, 2012) 85.
5. See Frank D. Macchia, "Sighs Too Deep for Words: Towards a Theology of Glossolalia," *Journal of Pentecostal Theology 1* (1992): 47-73.
6. David H. C. Read, *Preaching About the Needs of Real People* (Philadelphia: Westminster, 1988) 80.
7. Whiteley, 112.
8. Richard Foster, *Celebration of Discipline: The Path to Spiritual Growth* (New York: Harper, 1978) 42.
9. Adele Calhoun, *Spiritual Disciples Handbook* (Downers Grove, Ill.: InterVarsity, 2005) 219.
10. George Maloney, *A Return to Fasting* (Pecos, N. Mex.: Dove, 1974) 5.
11. Ray H. Hughes, *Pentecostal Preaching* (Cleveland, Tenn.: Pathway, 1981) 88.
12. Thomas E. Trask, et al., *The Pentecostal Pastor: A Mandate for the 21st Century* (Springfield, Mo.: Zondervan, 1997) 28.
13. Gardner C. Taylor, *How Shall They Preach* (Elgin, Ill.: Progressive Baptist Publishing, 1977) 60.
14. Calhoun, 169.
15. B. E. Underwood, *Spiritual Gifts: Ministries and Manifestations* (Franklin Springs, Ga.: Advocate, 1984) 89.
16. James Forbes, *The Holy Spirit and Preaching* (Nashville: Abington, 1989) 164.
17. Vinson Synan, *Spirit-Empowered Christianity in the 21st Century* (Lake Mary, Fla.: Charisma House, 2011) 184.
18. Wayne L. Fehr and Donald R. Hands, *Spiritual Wellness for Clergy* (Bethesda, Md.: The Alban Institute, 2001) 61.
19. Fehr and Hands, 62.
20. Greg Heisler, *Spirit-Led Preaching: The Holy Spirit's Role in Sermon Preparation and Delivery.* (Nashville: Broadman, 2007) 79.
21. Fred Craddock, *Preaching* (Nashville: Abingdon, 1985) 212.
22. Wilson, 162.
23. Darius Salter, *What Really Matters in Ministry* (Grand Rapids: Baker, 1990) 80.
24. Ray Corsini, *The Dictionary of Psychology* (New York: Brunner Routledge, 2002) 493.

## Endnotes

25. Bryan Chapell, *Christ-Centered Preaching* (Grand Rapids: Baker, 2003) 29.
26. Wilson, 151.
27. Charles B. Bugg, *Preaching & Intimacy: Preparing the Message and the Messenger* (Macon, Ga.: Smyth & Helwys, 1999) 4.
28. William Willimon and Richard Lischer, *Concise Encyclopedia of Preaching* (Louisville, Ky.: Westminster, 1995) 500-502.
29. Hughes, 23.
30. Murray Frick, *Reaching the Back Row: Creative Approaches for High-Impact Preaching* (Loveland, Colo.: Group, 1999) 16.
31. Charles Fuller, *The Trouble With "Truth Through Personality"* (Eugene, Ore.: Wipfand and Stock, 2010) 3.
32. Stanley Horton and William Menzies, *Biblical Doctrines: A Pentecostal Perspective* (Springfield, Mo.: Logion, 1993) 148.
33. Whiteley, 135.
34. James Earl Massey, *The Burdensome Joy of Preaching* (Nashville: Abingdon, 1998) 13.
35. Len Sperry, *Transforming Self and Community: Revisioning Pastoral Counseling and Spiritual Direction* (Collegeville, Minn.: The Liturgical Press, 2002) 96-97.

### Chapter 10

1. Thomas G. Long, *Preaching From Memory to Hope* (Louisville: John Knox Press, 2009) 33.
2. *Zeitgeist* is a German word that means "the spirit (*Geist*) of the time (*Zeit*)" and refers to the intellectual and cultural climate of an era; *es.wikipedia.org/wiki/Zeitgeist.*
3. Long, 67.
4. Alicia León León, Campus Digital; 2008; *um.es/campusdigital/Breves/ecuatorianos.htm.*
5. Humberto Giannini, *La Reflexión Cotidiana: Hacia una Arqueología de la Experiencia* (Chile: Editorial Universitaria, *1987) 31.*
6. Jorge Maldonado and Juan F. Martínez, eds., *Vivir y Servir en el Exilio,* FTL 29 (Buenos Aires: KAIROS, 2008) 28. In this book, Dr. Carlos Van Engen makes an excellent biblical-theological contribution on immigrants and foreigners in the *missio Dei* (mission of God).

### Chapter 11

1. Ray H. Hughes, *Pentecostal Preaching* (Cleveland, Tenn.: Church of God Department of General Education, 1981) 32-33.
2. Carl A. Volz, *Pastoral Life and Practice in the Early Church* (Minneapolis: Augsburg, 1990) 128.

3. Volz, 129.
4. Clyde E. Fant, *Bonhoeffer: Worldly Preaching* (Nashville: Nelson, 1975) 129.
5. Fant, 128.
6. Howard W. Stone, *The Word of God and Pastoral Care* (Nashville: Abingdon, 1988) 73.
7. Fant, 125.
8. Fant, 127.
9. Steven J. Land, *Pentecostal Spirituality: A Passion for the Kingdom*, JPTSup 1 (Sheffield, England: Sheffield Academic Press, 1993) 129.
10. John R. Claypool, *The Preaching Event* (Waco, Texas: Word Books, 1980) 28, 119.
11. Daniel E. Albrecht, *Rites in the Spirit: A Ritual Approach to Pentecostal/Charismatic Spirituality* (Sheffield, England: Sheffield Academic Press, 1999) 199.
12. Leslie C. Allen, *A Liturgy of Grief: A Pastoral Commentary on Lamentations* (Grand Rapids: Baker Academic, 2011) 11.
13. Allen, 12.
14. Friedrich Schleiermacher, James O. Duke, and Howard W. Stone, *Christian Caring: Selections From Practical Theology* (Philadelphia: Fortress, 1988) 109.
15. Schleiermacher, Duke, and Stone, 111-113.
16. Randy L. Maddox, *Responsible Grace: John Wesley's Practical Theology* (Nashville: Kingswood, 1994) 113.
17. Ray Sherman Anderson, *The Shape of Practical Theology: Empowering Ministry With Theological Praxis* (Downers Grove, Ill.: InterVarsity, 2001) 72.
18. Dorothy C. Bass, *Practicing Our Faith: A Way of Life for a Searching People* (San Francisco, Calif.: Jossey-Bass, 1997) 97-98.

### Conclusion

1. Daniel E. Albrecht, "Pentecostal Spirituality: Looking Through the Lens of Ritual," *Pneuma* 14.2 (1992): 110 (emphasis in the original).
2. R. Jerome Boone, "Community and Worship: The Key Components of Pentecostal Christian Formation," *Journal of Pentecostal Theology* 8 (1996): 137.
3. Allan Anderson, *An Introduction to Pentecostalism: Global Charismatic Christianity* (Cambridge, UK: Cambridge UP, 2004) 11.
4. Boone, 129-42.
5. Alice Reynolds Flower, "My Pentecost," *Assemblies of God Heritage* 20 (Winter 1997-98): 17-20; excerpted from her *Grace for Grace: Some*

*Highlights of God's Grace in the Daily Life of the Flower Family* (Springfield, Mo.: privately published, 1961).

6. Cited by Edith Waldvogel Blumhofer, "Pentecost in My Soul": *Explorations in the Meaning of Pentecostal Experience in the Assemblies of God* (Springfield, Mo.: Gospel Publishing, 1989) 159.

7. Chris E. W. Green, *Toward a Pentecostal Theology of the Lord's Supper: Foretasting the Kingdom* (Cleveland, Tenn.: CPT Press, 2012) 289 (emphasis in the original).

8. Rebecca Jaichandran and B. D. Madhav, "Pentecostal Spirituality in a Postmodern World," *Asian Journal of Pentecostal Studies* 6.1 (2003): 55.

9. *The Apostolic Faith* 1.1 (Sept. 1906): 1 and *passim*. William MacDonald, "Temple Theology," *Pneuma* 1.1 (Spring 1979): 48, insists, "Unless we dare claim that Christianity was fossilized in the first century, we must contend that the Spirit is still speaking to the churches." Cf. Cecil M. Robeck, *The Azusa Street Mission and Revival: The Birth of the Global Pentecostal Movement* (Nashville: Nelson Reference & Electronic, 2006) 132.

10. Keith Warrington, *Pentecostal Theology: A Theology of Encounter* (New York: T & T Clark, 2008) 219. Cf. Daniel E. Albrecht, *Rites in the Spirit: A Ritual Approach to Pentecostal/Charismatic Spirituality* (JPTSup, 17: Sheffield, UK: Sheffield Academic Press, 1999) 226, 38-39.

11. Boone, 138.

12. See Lee Roy Martin, "Longing for God: Psalm 63 and Pentecostal Spirituality," *Journal of Pentecostal Theology* 22.1 (April 2013): 54-76.

13. Johnathan E. Alvarado, "Worship in the Spirit: Pentecostal Perspectives on Liturgical Theology and Praxis," *Journal of Pentecostal Theology* 21.1 (2012): 143.